Assessing Gifted and Talented Children

Papers presented at an international seminar, London, February 2001

Qualifications and Curriculum Authority

First published in 2002
This collection is copyright © Qualifications and Curriculum Authority 2002
Copyright in the individual chapters remains with the chapter authors.

British Library Cataloguing-in-Publication Data
A catalogue record for this book is available from the British Library.

Printed in Great Britain.

The Qualifications and Curriculum Authority is an exempt charity under Schedule 2 of the Charities Act 1993.

Qualifications and Curriculum Authority
83 Piccadilly
London W1J 8QA
www.qca.org.uk

Compiled and edited by Carolyn Richardson Publishing Services.

Design by Rob Stephen.

Index compiled by Frank Pert.

ISBN: 1 85838 490 7

Contents

List of figures

List of tables

List of contributors

Randy Elliot Bennett is Distinguished Presidential Appointee at the Educational Testing Service (ETS) in Princeton, New Jersey, USA. He has conducted research on the applications of technology to testing and teaching, new forms of assessment and the assessment of children with disabilities. He has also researched the presentation and scoring of open-ended test items on the computer, the use of multimedia in testing and automated item generation. The author of many publications, including a monograph on large-scale educational testing, Randy Bennett is currently co-directing a series of studies on computerised testing for the US National Assessment of Educational Progress.

Hugh Burkhardt leads the task design and development work of MARS, the Mathematics Assessment Resource Service (University of Nottingham, UK, and Michigan State University, USA). He is a theoretical elementary-particle physicist and applied mathematician with an interest in improving teaching and learning. Having held appointments at various other universities in the UK and the USA, he joined the University of Nottingham in 1976 as Professor of Mathematical Education and Director of the Shell Centre. Since then he has led an international research team that develops tools for assessment, curriculum, professional development and other aspects of schools system improvement; World Class Tests are a major project at present.

Ron Casey is a Co-Director and Senior Research Fellow of the Brunel Able Children's Education Centre (BACE) at Brunel University, UK. Development projects he is currently involved in include an Urban Scholars Programme, development of subject specific models for provision for gifted pupils and the introduction of Critical Thinking courses for very able pupils. An experienced teacher, his main research interests are aspects of intelligence, creativity, talent search and development in children within inner-city areas and curriculum provision in secondary schools. He has written several books and papers on effective provision for able children.

Janice Curry is Research Officer at the Assessment and Evaluation Unit (AEU), University of Leeds, UK, and is currently developing mathematics tests for World Class Tests. She has nine years' UK teaching experience. She also has experience of providing in-service teacher training overseas, and was involved in extending the mathematical experience of able students in a secondary school. In 1995 she contributed to a national conference exploring under-performance by girls in Malawi. At the AEU she has developed materials for key stage 2 national tests and the National Numeracy Project, and has investigated the performance of English pupils in TIMSS.

Rosalind Elder has been Manager of the Gifted Education Research, Resource and Information Centre (GERRIC), University of New South Wales, Sydney, Australia, since 1996. Since her appointment she has overseen the establishment of six new programmes for gifted and talented children, including the Australian Primary Talent

Search (APTS), which has been operating since 1998. She is the editor of a series of curriculum units for gifted and talented students.

E. Jean Gubbins is Associate Professor of Educational Psychology at the University of Connecticut, USA, and Associate Director of the National Research Center on the Gifted and Talented. E. Jean Gubbins is a former classroom teacher and teacher of the gifted. In addition to her teaching experience with elementary and secondary students, she has been an instructor at college level, a consultant on gifted and talented education throughout the country, and an evaluator for the state department. She has published extensively.

Paul Kimmelman is a Special Advisor to the Executive Director at the North Central Regional Education Laboratory, USA, and Senior Consultant to Project 2061 of the American Association for the Advancement of Science. He was a member of the US National Commission on Mathematics and Science Teaching for the 21st Century and the TIMSS Technical Review Panel. A former teacher, Paul Kimmelman has also served as adjunct professor at several universities and acted as a consultant on school improvement and organisational transformation. He worked with QCA on the World Class Tests project and is co-authoring a book on transforming schools to world-class performance.

Valsa Koshy is a Co-Director and Reader in Education at the Brunel Able Children's Education Centre (BACE) at Brunel University, UK, with responsibility for the school-based elements of the Centre's work. She co-ordinates pupils' programmes and teacher-support courses with a network of Local Education Authorities (LEAs) across the country. She is head of the Academic and Professional Development programmes within the Department of Education, where she specialises in Primary education. Her research interests are the identification of gifted and talented pupils, mathematics education, assessment, and the impact of special programmes for gifted pupils. Valsa Koshy has published widely.

Gabrielle Matters is Director of the New Basics Branch, Education Queensland, Australia, leading the trial of an integrated framework for curriculum, pedagogy and assessment in Years 1 to 9. In 1986 she joined the Queensland Board of Studies, as a member of the tertiary entrance taskforce. As Deputy Director she headed the division responsible for the Queensland Core Skills Test for Year 12 students. An experienced teacher and Deputy Principal, Gabrielle Matters is the author of papers on test design and marking, and on the underachievement of boys; she has also written a book on test preparation.

Hilary Persky works with a team that coordinates the US National Assessment of Educational Progress (NAEP) arts and writing assessments, and leads one unit of a team that creates technology-based assessments. Before working for NAEP, she was an assisstant examiner for Verbal Admissions at Educational Testing Service (ETS), where she developed reading comprehension items for the Law School Admissions Test, the Graduate Records Examination (GRE), and the Graduate Management Admissions Test. She also developed items for the GRE Subject Test in world history and Praxis social studies test. Previously, she acted as NAEP assistant coordinator of US history and geography.

Peter Pool is Research Officer at the Assessment and Evaluation Unit (AEU), University of Leeds, UK. He spent 10 years teaching mathematics in UK schools, and eight years in teacher training and curriculum development work. He has also held numerous consultancies in six different countries around the world. A former PGCE mathematics tutor at the University of Oxford, he has seven years' experience of developing national statutory test materials for mathematics at key stage 2 and curriculum materials for the National Numeracy Project. Currently he is involved in the development of mathematics tests for QCA's World Class Tests.

Martin Ripley is Principal Manager of the New Projects Team at the Qualifications and Curriculum Authority (UK), which is currently developing a national Baseline Assessment Scheme (for five year olds), ICT tests for the statutory assessment programme, World Class Tests, and tests of Basic and Key Skills. After graduating from Harvard University, Martin taught in Chicago and Shanghai. Since 1991 he has worked on England's national statutory assessment and test development project. He managed the development of English, mathematics and science tests for seven, 11 and 14 year olds and created a national system for providing evaluative annual feedback to schools.

Linda Jensen Sheffield is Regent's Professor at North Kentucky University, USA, where she holds a joint appointment in the School of Education and the Department of Mathematics and Computer Science. She chaired the NCTM Task Force on Mathematically Promising Students and was editor of the NCTM book, *Developing Mathematically Promising Students*. She was Chief Organiser of the Working Group for Action for Mathematics Education in Pre- and Primary School at the Ninth International Congress of Mathematics Education in Japan and is currently working on the NCTM *Navigations* series of books to accompany the new Principles and Standards.

Diane Shorrocks-Taylor, of the Assessment and Evaluation Unit (AEU), University of Leeds, UK, has many years' experience in education and teacher training. She has directed major national projects, including the Evaluation of National Curriculum Assessment (1992), the development of the national statutory test materials in mathematics at key stage 2 1992–2000 and the development of materials for the National Numeracy Project. She is currently directing the development of the mathematics tests for QCA's World Class Tests project. She has published widely in the area of assessment and evaluation.

Gordon Stobart is Senior Lecturer in Assessment at the University of London Institute of Education, UK. After working as a secondary school teacher he retrained as an educational psychologist. Later, after studying in the USA as a Fulbright Scholar, he moved into research, becoming Head of Research at London Examinations at the time of the introduction of GCSE. He moved on to become Principal Research Officer in Assessment at the National Council for Vocational Qualifications, where he was involved in the development of GNVQ. He subsequently transferred to QCA, where he worked on national tests and examinations.

Bronwen Swinnerton is a Research Fellow at the Assessment and Evaluation Unit (AEU), University of Leeds, UK. She has worked on a number of projects commissioned by QCA, including research into the performance of English pupils in TIMSS; an investigation assessing higher levels of attainment in mathematics at key stage 2; key stage 2 performance analysis in 1997; the 1999 performance analysis of mathematics at key stage 1, Years 3, 4 and 5 optional tests and key stage 2. Currently she is involved in the development of mathematics tests for QCA's World Class Tests project, and has particular responsibility for research methods.

Acknowledgements

Chapter 1: For the examples of problem-solving tasks reproduced in this chapter, Hugh Burkhardt expresses his gratitude to the MARS team, particularly Malcolm Swan, Jim Ridgway, Rita Crust and Alan Bell.

Chapter 2: Randy Elliot Bennett and Hilary Persky would like to thank the Educational Testing Service staff members who have contributed to the Problem Solving in Technology-Rich Environments project, including Malcolm Bauer, Kevin Bentley, Jeff Haberstroh, Cindy Hammell, Kathy Howell, Frank Jenkins, Holly Knott, Mary Lauko, Lou Mang, Chris O'Sullivan, Debbie Pisacreta and Peggy Redman.

Chapter 3: Gabrielle Matters would like to acknowledge the staff of the New Basics Branch, Education Queensland: Tony Cook, Kirran Follers, Ken Gray, Ezette Grauf, Paul Herschell, Peter Lloyd, Cath O'Hara, Nola Simpson and Anna van Hoof.

Chapter 4: Peter Pool expresses his gratitude to colleagues at the Assessment and Evaluation Unit at the University of Leeds, who so freely gave their insights into the development of questions, and to children who took part in trials of materials, who so freely gave their thoughts.

Chapter 5: Diane Shorrocks-Taylor, Bronwen Swinnerton and Janice Curry would like to thank Mick Quinlan at QCA for his help in gaining access to some of the data used in this chapter.

Chapter 6: Linda Jensen Sheffield would like to thank Scott Trimble and the staff at the Kentucky Department of Education for all their assistance in the data collection.

Chapter 7: E. Jean Gubbins would like to acknowledge Dr Joseph S. Renzulli, University of Connecticut, Storrs, USA. In 1990 he proposed a vision for the National Research Center on the Gifted and Talented; he truly believed that the Center could create a research agenda that would have an impact on identification and programming procedures throughout the country. The Center is currently implementing its third, five-year federally funded grant from the United States Department of Education, Office of Educational Research and Improvement, and its research findings are acknowledged throughout the world.

Chapter 8: Ron Casey and Valsa Koshy wish to acknowledge all the children who took the test trials with so much enthusiasm and provided the data for this chapter.

Chapter 9: Rosalind Elder would like to thank Professor Miraca Gross, Dr Katherine Hoekman and the staff of the Gifted Education Research, Resource and Information Centre, Sydney, Australia for their tireless work in promoting the special needs of gifted children to the community.

Foreword

Michael Barber
Prime Minister's Delivery Unit, London, UK

WORLD CLASS TESTS ARE A KEY ELEMENT in the UK Government's strategy for gifted and talented children and will act as a benchmark to ensure that pupils educated in England are on a par with the best worldwide. They will also be in the vanguard of responding to some new and rapidly evolving influences that will transform our education system over the coming decades.

The first of these influences is technology, which will have a profound effect on the educational experience of future generations. Children now have access to an extraordinary range of technology and are developing new forms of communication – beginning but not ending with text messaging! Technological developments will also soon revolutionise their experience of the classroom and of teaching.

The second influence is globalisation. Our young people look ahead to a life in which not only the job market but also the range of challenges facing them are global in character. The curriculum needs to reflect this reality, above all, in the standards it sets. Whilst history may vary from country to country, algebra is algebra and physics is physics. Only if our young people match the standards of their peers elsewhere will they be able to play a full part in the global economy of the future. As we look to other countries it becomes clear that, in terms of curriculum, there is much that we can learn from each other. Increasingly, countries will come to take common educational expectations for granted and then reap the benefit of being able to exchange ideas and findings across national boundaries more readily. This exchange of information will increasingly occur at the level of the classroom and the teacher as well in policy-making and academic circles.

The third set of influences concerns the future direction of national curricula. Schools in England are already treating the national curriculum as a basic minimum level of provision and many are moving beyond it to provide a much broader range of opportunities and learning experiences for their pupils. Increasingly, schools are seeking to identify their most able pupils and to make separate and distinctive provision for those pupils.

It is the task of the New Projects Team at the Qualifications and Curriculum Authority to design an entirely new testing and assessment system that responds to the three sets of developments I have outlined above. That is what they, working with others, have done in producing World Class Tests. The tests are about assessing children's computer-based cognition, skills and understandings – three areas that we are only just beginning to research and understand. Much of our experience in England over the past eight years has shown how powerful and influential it can be to have a commonly used set of tests. The World Class Tests will create a shared experience with teachers from around the world, which will enable us all to take forward the debate about how to teach most effectively and to identify which schools are better at this than others and why. This in turn will make information available to schools about the relative impacts of teaching and culture; it will also pave the way to understanding how we can all do better.

World Class Tests began with the idea of designing tests in mathematics and problem solving for nine and 13 year old children. Already QCA has extended that idea by beginning to produce related teaching and learning materials. I have no doubt that the project will continue to extend its work – perhaps into other subject and cognitive areas, perhaps more generally across the ability range and probably into non-English forms of test provision. As I write this Foreword, the first live administration of World Class Tests has not yet taken place, but teachers from other countries involved in QCA's pilot project have already seen the potential of the tests.

I am pleased to be able to introduce this book, which is QCA'S first volume of research and thinking from around the world about assessing gifted and talented students.

London, August 2001.

Introduction

Martin Ripley
Qualifications and Curriculum Authority, London, UK

No MODERN EGALITARIAN SOCIETY can (or should) function without ensuring that *all* its young people are given the maximum opportunity to develop their skills and understanding. Much attention has rightly been given to ensuring educational access and inclusion for those children who are in some way disadvantaged. But recently there has been re-emerging interest in challenging the brightest students in our schools. One of the most visionary ideas for meeting the needs of these students is the idea of World Class Tests for nine and 13 year old children – as outlined in the policy document, *Excellence in Cities*, produced by the UK Government in March 1999 (DfEE, 1999).

In February 2001, the Qualifications and Curriculum Authority (QCA) was honoured to host a conference which brought together some of the people working in this area. The papers published in this book reflect the commitment of the UK Government to the field of provision for gifted and talented children as well as providing an excellent opportunity to advance our collective understanding in areas of assessment, use of technology and international co-operation.

World Class Tests

The major elements underpinning the idea of the new World Class Arena are that the World Class Tests developed should be
- tests of mathematics and problem solving;
- aimed at the top 10 per cent (in ability terms) of students internationally;
- aimed primarily at students of nine and 13 years of age;
- computer based, where this is educationally viable;
- internationally calibrated to provide teachers with comparative information in relation to the performance of students in other countries;
- widely available, throughout the world, for students to take whenever they are ready;
- supported by other learning, teaching and assessment materials designed to aid teachers and parents in preparing students for the tests.

However, the philosophy and educational ideas reflected by the tests embrace a number of considerations. First, these tests represent a significant development in educational policy in England: schools are expected to identify the needs of their most able students and to provide for the needs of those students. In other words, each school is expected to identify it own highest achieving students and, in terms of the relative abilities of students within the school, to provide a distinctive programme for the most able. Second, the launch of World Class Tests reflects a wish to improve England's relative international performance – as exemplified through the TIMSS and TIMSS-R studies (see Harris *et al*, 1997, Keys *et al*, 1996, Ruddock, 2000). Third, it is also intended that the tests, together with teaching and learning materials that will underpin them, will be a means of measuring the extent to which the performance of our most able students is improving over time. Fourth, the tests reflect a view that computer technology can be harnessed to design and develop worthwhile and valuable assessment activities at the same time as delivering other benefits, such as improving the speed of marking and providing improved accessibility for students.

In meeting this agenda, the tests have four key purposes.

1. **To identify and recognise the achievements of students.**
    This reflects the intrinsic value to the student (and parents) of his or her achievement in the tests.

2. **To provide guidance to schools and teachers on the standards to be expected of the most able students.**
    We will be producing teaching and learning materials to support the tests. In addition, the tests themselves will help schools understand the sorts of skills, understanding and knowledge that their most able students should be taught as well as the standards of performance that can be expected of them.

3. **To provide schools with guidance about the standards expected of the most able students in other countries.**
    The tests will reflect standards and expectations of the top 10 per cent of students internationally. The domains for the tests and the content of the tests are designed to reflect this vision – test questions, question contexts, assumed and tested knowledge and standards of performance are designed to reflect this international context.

4. **To provide schools with information about how well their students are performing in relation to other countries.**
    Building on the above, the final purpose is that of providing information on test results to schools in such a form that teachers (and parents) can readily make internationally comparable judgements about their students' performance.

KEY CHALLENGES

In seeking to meet the challenge and potential of these exciting ideas, we have formed a partnership in England involving two other organisations – AQA (the Assessment and Qualifications Alliance, which has extensive examinations experience) and Doublestruck (an educational software supplier). This partnership is shaping the future by identifying key challenges which must be met if the idea of World Class Tests is to be successful.

First, the partnership must provide useful educational materials for schools, not just tests. Indeed, the tests will become of secondary importance in meeting the aims of providing challenging educational material for gifted and talented children and of providing materials drawn from teaching styles and educational cultures which differ in many ways between countries. The work of James Stigler and James Hiebert (Stigler and Hiebert, 1999) begins to show how important and deep-seated are the differences in the ways in which teachers from different countries teach and instruct their students. As we write learning material and test questions designed to be reflective of the classroom instructional practices found in the best performing schools and countries, we will find that our work starts to highlight some of the features identified by Stigler and Hiebert.

Second, our learning and assessment materials will harness some of the most advanced technology capable of supporting the provision of teaching, learning and assessment materials for schools. In our work to date in developing World Class Test assessment material, we have found teachers expecting some bonus from the provision of assessment materials on screen. Often, we have found that teachers' expectations are that technology should favourably alter the assessment experience for the child – this has been as (technically) straightforward as providing a voice-over facility on our materials. It has also, however, informed our entire approach to the design of computer-based assessment materials. Almost all of our screen-based test questions are reflective of assessments that could not take place on paper. We have also found children to be genuinely excited and motivated by the materials.

These reactions have not been confined to England. A teacher in Argentina told us:

My first reaction was one of distrust… Why does the UK want to examine students from other countries? I found the exercises in the tests very interesting. The feeling of distrust vanished.

(Business Planning and Research International, 2000)

The World Class Arena project – especially the teaching, learning and assessment materials it produces – raises fundamental issues about key aspects of our work.

• What intelligences are children using when they work on computer, think on computer and respond to computer-stimulated problems?
• Which parts of this work are unique to the needs of gifted and talented children?
• How might the idea of cross-national exchanges of educational material work?

The QCA seminar, February 2001

These, and other issues, formed the basis of an international seminar held in London in February 2001. The seminar consisted of a range of presentations, discussions and workshop sessions and it is the intention of this book to provide to a wider audience a flavour of the discussions that took place.

The keynote speaker was Michael Barber, then head of the Standards and Effectiveness Unit in England. He described how two threads of change – internationalism and technological advancement – are already beginning to influence the ways in which we think about the curriculum and the ways in which education can be organised. Nowhere are these threads more clearly at work than in the ideas underpinning World Class Tests. Those themes are developed in the Foreword to this book.

Part I (page 5) takes the assessment of problem-solving as its theme. The chapters in this section explore the question, 'What is problem-solving?' Hugh Burkhardt's chapter argues that problem-solving ability consists of a range of skills, some of which might be domain specific. The assessment of that ability involves the presentation to students of a range of new (that is, previously unseen) problems which are themselves worthwhile problems to solve. As with the chapter by Randy Elliot Bennett and Hilary Persky, the model of problem-solving discussed in this book involves extensive use of computers to provide models and simulations for students.

Part II (page 51) takes the assessment of the mathematical abilities and understandings of gifted and talented children as its theme. The chapters by Peter Pool and Diane Shorrocks-Taylor *et al.* are based on empirical data emerging directly from the development of World Class Tests and from schools in England that have been working extensively with us over the past 18 months. The chapter by Linda Jensen Sheffield outlines the approach to assessment and identification taken in Northern Kentucky, one of the states most clearly pursuing a standards driven-policy.

Part III (page 93) takes three specific issues from an assessment perspective. I am grateful to my former colleague, Gordon Stobart – now at the Institute of Education, University of London – for providing an overview of this section. The chapter by Ron Casey and Valsa Koshy puts forward compelling data to support the view that gifted and talented children exist in many or all schools and that one of the key challenges to educators is to find ways of recognising and encouraging that talent, particularly when it is expressed in non-academic means. This paper, published for the first time here, has already featured in several newspaper articles in England. The chapters by E. Jean Gubbins and Rosalind Elder provide a wider perspective on the assessment of gifted and talented children, looking at some of the reasons for such assessments to be used.

Finally, I am grateful to all the colleagues who attended and participated in the seminar in February 2001, including Eva Baker and Harry O'Neil, both of whom led presentations at the seminar. Particular thanks go to Jeremy Tafler, Lorna D'Arcy, Jon Waldren, George Vassiadis, Sladana Krstic, Alison Brittan, Nicole Magnier and Katy Pugh, who have worked on the World Class Tests project at QCA and who organised the seminar in February 2001.

London, August 2001.

As you read through this book, please refer as necessary to the Appendices (pages 127 to 130) for details on the education systems of the UK, USA and Australia.

4

PART I

The Assessment of Problem-Solving Skills

Overview

Hugh Burkhardt

Mathematics Assessment Resource Service (MARS) University of Nottingham, UK, and Michigan State University, USA

Problem solving has long been recognised as a key element in performance – in most school subjects as in life itself. One's education is incomplete without the ability to adapt existing knowledge and skills to tasks and situations that are significantly different from those studied in school. The best teachers of the gifted and talented have always challenged students with non-routine tasks that require them to construct, rather than merely remember, long chains of reasoning involving connections that are new to them. Since the 1950s, such work has become part of the intended curriculum in many subjects taught in many different countries: the UK, the US, Australia and the Netherlands have been among the pioneers, whilst Japan, Taiwan and other Far Eastern systems are increasingly moving in this direction. Enquiry-based approaches to learning science, investigative work in mathematics, and the emphasis on design in the technology curriculum are all examples of this.

Assessment has sometimes made an important contribution by recognising and rewarding problem-solving performance. The introduction of coursework into the UK GCSE examination is one example; it requires students to produce a portfolio of extended pieces of work, which are assessed and included in their final score, along with the marks on timed written tests. Generally, however, high-stakes assessment of problem solving has lagged behind the curriculum developments, and so inhibited their large-scale implementation.

The reasons for this are both developmental and institutional. The design and development of assessment for higher-level skills like problem solving *is* more challenging than for the recall of facts and learned procedures. More powerful development methods are needed, and these are one focus of Part I of this book. The institutional barriers vary from place to place. The US assessment tradition has an emphasis on carefully trialled short items that assess one specific thing in isolation – but problem solving is largely about extended chains of reasoning, in which the different elements interact strongly with each other. In the UK, in contrast, the tasks in the high-stakes examinations are often much longer. However, there is usually no opportunity for trialling tasks; they are drafted by a principal examiner then, without any student responses, they are discussed, revised and approved by a committee. Those involved rightly feel responsible to the community of teachers whose students will take the examination. It is not surprising that the tasks that emerge are minor variants of those set in previous years, all of which will be practised by students preparing for the examination. In all systems, there are such pressures to make the assessment *'routine'*; an active countervailing *'engine for improvement'* is thus a system element that is essential for the sustained assessment of problem solving.

The chapters in Part I discuss these challenges in three complementary ways. In Chapter 1, I give a broad outline of principles that underlie the assessment of problem solving, and the roles it can play in education. The discussion is illustrated with some assessment tasks and includes a section on specifying an assessment domain in a useful way, which complements the task set.

In Chapter 2, by contrast, Randy Bennett and Hilary Persky, from the Educational Testing Service in Princeton, describe in some detail the form and development of a single problem-solving task. This task offers a technology-rich environment to students, through which they can explore the buoyancy of a gas balloon, using skills in both scientific enquiry and computer technology. The scope and refinement of the development methodology are a notable feature.

In Chapter 3, Gabrielle Matters describes a specific initiative that is broad in both scope and ambition. The State of Queensland has a well-developed tradition of externally-monitored school-based assessment. The Rich Tasks are an exciting and challenging new approach, broader in many ways than what has been tried elsewhere. Each task embraces a transdisciplinary range of knowledge, skills and problem solving in a focussed project format.

A notable feature of all three chapters is that all the tasks, though assessment is their prime focus, also enable the students who take part to engage in high-quality learning experiences – and thus provide a stimulus to the curriculum.

1 World Class assessment: principles, practice and problem solving

Hugh Burkhardt

Mathematics Assessment Resource Service (MARS) University of Nottingham, UK, and Michigan State University, USA

THE ASSESSMENT OF PROBLEM SOLVING epitomises all the problems of designing and developing high quality assessment. Indeed, any test that goes beyond the routine assesses problem solving, in some sense of the phrase. Most assessment claims to cover more than learned facts and procedures in familiar contexts, although the tasks the students are asked to do (and the aspects of performance rewarded in the scoring schemes) often show these claims to be unfounded. Similarly, the assessment of gifted and talented children simply highlights more general problems. Clearly, mundane and narrow assessment tasks are not good enough for these children; neither should they be for any child.

An introduction to problem solving

To summarise the essentials of problem solving:
- a 'problem' is non-routine, in some sense an unfamiliar task;
- the solver must *find*, not just remember, the path to a solution.

So beyond 'the basics', everything is problem solving, though the degree of unfamiliarity (the *transfer distance*) will vary. The theme of this chapter will be the central importance of:
- the richness of the tasks on which students are assessed;
- the range, variety and balance of the task set, sampled in each test.

With this as a theme, examples are essential. Those presented here are mostly from MARS work on developing tasks for World Class Tests and for other projects. They are simplified to save space, sometimes by removing some of the 'scaffolding' that helps give students access to the problem. A rich collection of tasks can be found in the

For brief notes on the UK and US education systems, please see pages 127 and 128.

balanced assessment packages (Balanced Assessment, 1998) and the tests for students aged nine to 16 (MARS, 2000), which the team has developed. Here I am particularly indebted to Malcolm Swan, Jim Ridgeway, Rita Crust and Alan Bell. More about MARS' work, including references, can be found at www.educ.msu.edu/MARS/.

The examples will run parallel to the text. They are mainly from the area in which we have most experience: mathematics in the broadest sense, with an emphasis on solving substantial problems, many involving the application of mathematics in practical situations. This is now the standard view of mathematics in the international community and in the UK national curricula, at least in principle; in practice, various assessment and curriculum pressures have produced sharp narrowing. The examples here are all of paper-based tasks; the computer-based tasks, which I cannot show here, are one of the most exciting features of the World Class Tests project (see the QCA website www.qca.org.uk/ca/tests/wct/, for some examples).

'Design a Tent' (Figure 1.1) is a good example to start with. It is a mathematics task, and a problem solving task, with a strong flavour of design technology. It is a problem of obvious practical relevance and is the kind of design task that we all need to be able to think through – if only to take a critical look at designs with which we are presented. For the moment, please just work out how you would do the task; we shall comment further later.

Figure 1.1: *'Design a Tent' task (for 14 to 16 year olds)*

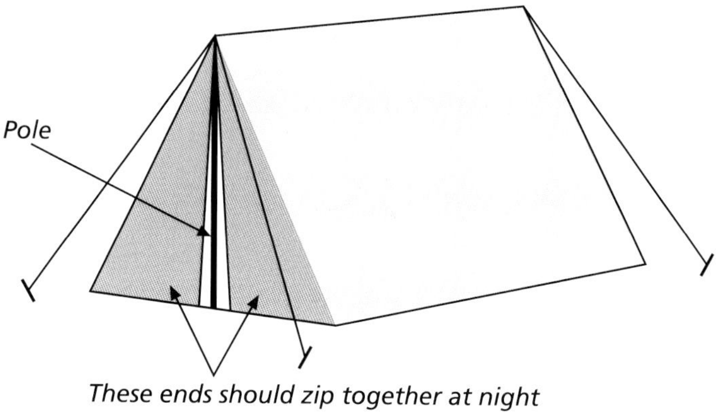

Pole

These ends should zip together at night

Your task is to design a tent like the one in the picture.
Your design must satisfy these conditions

- It must be big enough for two adults to sleep in (with their baggage).
- It must be big enough for someone to move around in while kneeling down.
- The bottom of the tent will be made from a thick rectangle of plastic.
- The sloping sides and the two ends will be made from a single, large sheet of canvas. (It should be possible to cut the canvas so that the two ends do not need sewing onto the sloping sides. It should be possible to zip up the ends at night.)
- Two vertical poles will hold the tent up.

Principles in the design of problem solving tasks

The development of good assessment tasks is one of the most challenging aspects of educational design. The teacher observation and targeted guidance that characterise good lessons cannot be used. The tasks have to work on their own, allowing students to show what they know, understand and can do across the domain.

I will outline some principles for designing and developing high-quality assessment, some of the difficulties that arise in practice, and how the reductions in quality they tend to produce may be minimised. This may suggest familiar ground, and I hope that much of what I say will indeed seem obvious. However, I choose it because the quality of so much of the assessment that children face around the world is undermined by neglecting the 'obvious'. There are often 'sound, practical reasons' adduced for this: 'We don't know how to do that', 'It won't be reliable enough', 'It's all too complicated', 'It will cost too much', and so on.

These are real challenges, but assessment design – like good design in any field – is about finding attractive ways around such obstructions within the constraints that every problem involves. Modern aircraft, for example, are significantly more comfortable, faster and safer, than the Wright brothers' prototype though all the objections listed above were applicable. In assessment design, as in every other field, we can do better.

In MARS' work for all its client systems, we are seeking high quality in this sense. In developing World Class Tests, there are some interesting new challenges. MARS' experience is largely in mathematics; the assessment of problem solving in mathematics, science and technology presents even broader challenges of task design and domain definition. We are making progress with these but there is much still to learn. The same can be said about the design and marking of computer-based tasks although, because of the complexities inherent in software development, we are not yet as far forward there. I mention these two exciting aspects of World Class Tests to make a more general point – that the development of assessment for problem solving is not a straightforward procedure. The design of assessment of skills beyond the routine cannot itself be routine.

THE VALIDITY PRINCIPLE
Assess what you want the student to be able to do

What could be simpler or more obvious than this first principle? The fundamental criterion for a good task is that it should be described by a well-educated non-specialist person as 'the kind of thing our children should be able to do'. 'Pollen' (Figure 1.2, page 10) meets this criterion and requires the student to use data analysis and scientific inference skills. Such data-based tasks often also involve evaluation and recommendation, with the student in a 'consultant' role.

Yet, in most assessment, such face validity is hard to find. Instead, you find tasks that imitate the exercises that students are given in the curriculum – a very different thing. Why? Neglect of the next principle is a major reason.

THE HOLISTIC PRINCIPLE
Assess samples, not ingredients, of performance

This links closely to the validity principle. It is widely ignored for the following attractive and plausible reason. Performance is made up of a limited set of separate 'ingredients'; if we assess each of these, we have assessed performance. These ingredients are sometimes listed as detailed behavioural objectives. In the original National Curriculum in mathematics for England, they were called 'statements of attainment'. The idea is to assess whether each student can, or cannot, do each of them: a simple and appealing concept.

Figure 1.2: *'Pollen' task (for 12 to 14 year olds)*

Each day newspapers print the temperature, the humidity and the number of pollen grains in a sample of air. This is to help people who suffer from hay fever.
Here are the figures for eight days:

DATE	TEMPERATURE (°C)	HUMIDITY (%)	NUMBER OF POLLEN GRAINS
16 May	26	58	80
1 June	24	49	148
23 June	25	66	25
7 July	17	45	170
9 July	20	42	210
20 July	19	34	258
2 August	25	30	304
23 August	22	46	173

From the information in the table, is the number of pollen grains in the air affected by humidity, temperature or both? How can you tell?

Describe any relationships you see.

However, it doesn't work for two major reasons. The first is that if the ingredients are to have a specific difficulty level, it turns out you need to specify them in great detail – not 'can multiply whole numbers' but 'can multiply a three-digit number by a two-digit number, set out in standard form, with carrying involved'. So you need thousands of separate assessment criteria, which becomes impracticable.

However, this is a relatively minor problem compared to the second reason, which relates to the 'composite task' effect. For a substantial task that involves a number of such elements of performance, the whole is much more than the sum of the parts. Assessing a student on each bit separately tells you little about how they would do on the task as a whole. If you want to see how good someone is at driving a car, would you carry out separate tests on starting the engine, turning the steering wheel and changing gear… or would you go for a drive with them? Performance on each separate ingredient does *not* tell you how well they can drive; assessing their driving as a whole *does* show whether they can perform all the component tasks.

'Design a Tent' (Figure 1.1, page 8) would be far a less valuable or plausible task if it were broken up into a sequence of steps such as: Estimate how tall a person might be. How much space should you leave for their baggage? How wide a sleeping space should you leave for each person? How tall should the tent be so they can move around kneeling? What are the dimensions of the base rectangle? Use the Pythagorean theorem to calculate the height of the sloping sides, and the dimensions of the triangular ends…

The essential point is to assess whether the student can handle the *strategy* as well as the *techniques* needed to solve the problem – can choose which tools to use, as well as using them reliably (like climbing a mountain without, or with, an expert guide).

Without experience of solving problems that are both unfamiliar and substantial, like those we face in daily life, our skills are of limited use. The national curriculum in mathematics recognises this fully in its principles but, though statements of attainment are long gone, the fragmentation they prescribed still dominates. To check on this, just look at the length of most of the assessment tasks – or rather, because they are often broken into many small parts, the length of the longest part of each task (which we call the *reasoning length*). For most mathematics assessment tasks, this is only a minute or two; how many significant real-life problems are as short as this?

THE WYTIWYG PRINCIPLE
Encourage curriculum balance
With high-stakes assessment, where the results have important consequences for those involved, What You Test Is What You Get in the classroom (hence WYTIWYG). So balanced assessment is a key principle for MARS (indeed it is the title of our first international project). The assessment designers' responsibility is to ensure that teachers who 'teach to the test' are led to provide a rich and balanced curriculum.

Teachers naturally emphasise those aspects of performance that are 'in the test'. They would be very brave (and perhaps irresponsible) not to, since society decrees that their students and their performance be judged by test results. So, in the language of the Third International Mathematics and Science Study (TIMSS), if the test does not cover the performance goals of the *intended curriculum*, the actual *implemented curriculum* will narrow to match the *tested curriculum*. In this way, unbalanced high-stakes assessment always distorts the curriculum.

In practice, this distortion often happens 'by accident', through lack of awareness. Thus when the Dearing Report (Dearing, 1994), in response to pressure, recommended the simplification of the key stage tests (see page 127), it also said that the missing areas should be covered by teacher assessment in the classroom, which should 'carry equal weight'. This second aspect was not achieved.

Problem solving, in any subject, is a frequent casualty of narrowing. Some believe that it is unfair or impossible to assess problem solving in a timed exam. But comparing students' performances on examination tasks, taking between five and 20 minutes, with other methods of assessment shows that it is possible to do it fairly. 'Snakes and Ladders' (see Figure 1.3, page 12) is a simple mathematical task that assesses important aspects of problem solving in the design process, particularly critique and improvement.

The importance of balance is such that I will reinforce the argument with an example from another field of assessment. Suppose your goal is to develop athletes for the decathlon, with the broad and balanced skills that this event requires. They train on 10 events and assessment takes two days, in a big stadium with lots of equipment and officials. Eventually someone comes up with the following line of reasoning:

> *We don't want to waste time on assessment; it's the training that matters. Let's keep it simple. Performance on the 100 metres is simple to measure and it's well correlated with general athletic ability. Good all-round athletes are usually pretty good at it. Great idea – we'll decide the winner of the decathlon with a 100-metre race!*

Do you think this might have some effect on the balance of training? This kind of absurdity happens unnoticed in many kinds of assessment – the tests students take cover only a small part of the range of things they are supposed to be learning. Soon the implemented curriculum shrinks to match the test.

Figure 1.3: *'Snakes and Ladders' task (for eight to 10 year olds)*

Read the following description of a game, then answer the questions below.

You will need a coin and two counters.

Rules

- Take it in turns to toss the coin. If it is heads, move your counter 2 places.
- If it is tails, move your counter 1 place.
- If you reach the foot of a ladder, you must go up it.
- If you reach the head of a snake, you must go down it.

1. List and describe all the faults you notice with the board above.

2. On this blank board, design a game using 4 snakes and 4 ladders which does not have the faults you found.

   Below are two further copies of the blank board in case you make a mistake.

   If you use more than one board, tick the one you think is best.

However, the balance principle is not just a challenge but also an opportunity. For various reasons, not simply because of narrow assessment, the curriculum in many classrooms is far narrower than the intended curriculum. When new types of task are introduced into high-stakes assessment, teachers will try to bring those new aspects of performance in the subject into their teaching. If they are to do it well, many will need help in the form of well-aligned teaching materials and professional development support. At the Shell Centre in Nottingham we developed this model in the 1980s with one of the national examining boards, introducing one new task type each year (Swan *et al*, 1984). The model worked well. Others have used a similar approach.

What is balance?

This is a huge topic, raising all kinds of issues, which I do not have space to go into here. Ultimately balance is a judgement for the professional peer group in the subject, guided by society at large. However, it is worth outlining the kind of analytic framework within which balance should be explored, for it is here that an assessment domain is defined.

I have emphasised the importance in designing tasks of a holistic approach, focused on worthwhile tasks rather than the separate elements of performance. But these elements are part of an analytic framework for defining the domain of assessment. It is in looking at balance that the analytic and holistic best come together. 'OK, so this is an attractive collection of tasks. Can you describe what they assess?'

The essential feature of a framework is that it should address *all* the aspects of performance that may be regarded as important. For this it must be multidimensional. A driving test must address the *technical* skills we have mentioned (such as steering). It must also be concerned with other *strategic* dimensions of performance (such as awareness of other

Table 1.1: *Dimensions of balance*

MATHEMATICAL CONTENT DIMENSION

- **Mathematical content** will include some of:
  Number and quantity including: concepts and representation; computation; estimation and measurement; number theory and general number properties.
  Algebra, patterns and function including: patterns and generalisation; functional relationships (including ratio and proportion); graphical and tabular representation; symbolic representation; forming and solving relationships.
  Geometry, shape and space including: shape, properties of shapes, relationships; spatial representation, visualisation and construction; location and movement; transformation and symmetry; trigonometry.
  Handling data, statistics and probability including: collecting, representing, interpreting data; probability models – experimental and theoretical; simulation.
  Other mathematics including: discrete mathematics, including combinatorics; underpinnings of calculus; mathematical structures.

MATHEMATICAL PROCESS DIMENSION

- **Phases** of problem solving, reasoning and communication will include, as broad categories, some or all of:
  modeling and formulating;
  transforming and manipulating;
  inferring and drawing conclusions;
  checking and evaluating;
  reporting.

TASK TYPE DIMENSIONS

- **Task type** will be one of: open investigation; non-routine problem; design; plan; evaluation and recommendation; review and critique; re-presentation of information; technical exercise; definition of concepts.
- **Non-routineness** in: context; mathematical aspects or results; mathematical connections.
- **Openness**: it may have an open end with open questions; open middle.
- **Type of goal** is one of: pure mathematics; illustrative application of the mathematics; applied power over the practical situation.
- **Reasoning length** is the expected time for the longest section of the task (It is an indication of the amount of 'scaffolding' – the detailed step-by-step guidance that the prompt may provide)

CIRCUMSTANCES OF PERFORMANCE DIMENSIONS

- **Task length**: ranging from short tasks (five to 15 minutes), through long tasks (15 to 60 minutes), to extended tasks (several days to several weeks)
- **Modes of presentation**: written; oral; video; computer.
- **Modes of working** on the task: individual; group; mixed.
- **Modes of response** by the student: written; built; spoken; programmed; performed.

road users) and how they all interact. The 'Dimensions of balance' in Table 1.1 summarise the framework MARS has developed for mathematics over the last decade. A parallel framework for problem solving in mathematics, science and technology is now being developed by MARS, with QCA and international experts, as part of the World Class Tests.

The first point of note is that the 'mathematical content' of concepts and skills is only one important dimension; to be balanced across content, which most tests are, is not enough to claim that one assesses performance in mathematics. What of the other dimensions of performance? Brief comments must suffice here. A detailed handbook, illustrated with many tasks, is available for those who want to know more (Bell and Burkhardt, 2000).

Task length and *reasoning length* have already been mentioned. Balance here is clearly important; if you want people to be able to sustain chains of reasoning longer than a minute or two, you must include an appropriate proportion of tasks that require it.

Process dimensions address the strategic and tactical aspects of performance – the exploring, planning, carrying through, reflecting on and communicating the solution to the task. These major *phases* are all essential elements in performance and should be substantially represented in any balanced test. Most mathematics assessment is unbalanced in this regard, with an overwhelming proportion of the *transforming and manipulating* aspect. (Better balance requires longer tasks.) One can analyse process aspects in much more detail; we do so for research purposes but it does not seem essential for balancing tests, where checking on all the dimensions is more important than going into great detail on any one.

The other dimensions also need attention in balancing. *Goal type* and *context* dimensions, for example, are there to identify the 'using and applying of mathematics'.

Figure 1.4: *'Rope' task (for 12 to 14 year olds)*

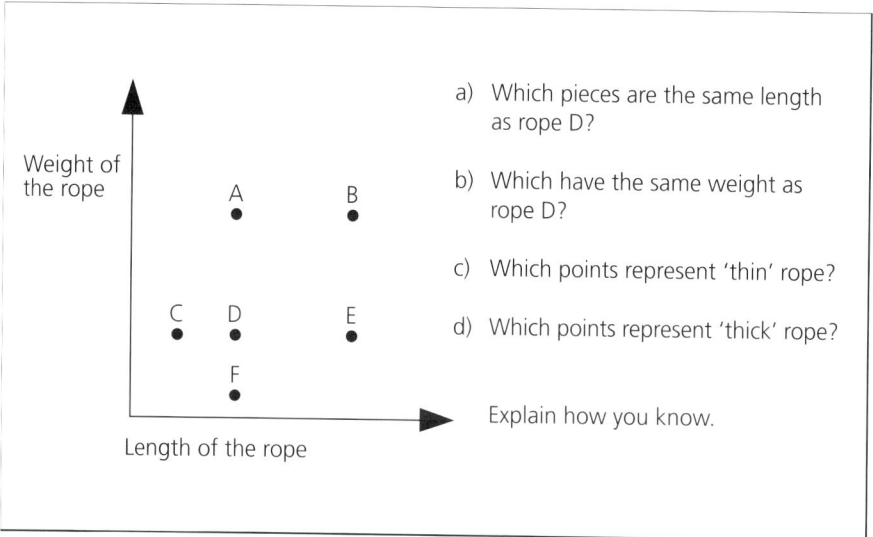

Finally, task type is a useful dimension of a slightly different kind, summarising combinations of the other aspects within a single task in a way that is easy to understand. The types listed represent important ways of doing mathematics. We have already seen examples of 'design' and 'plan' ('Design a Tent' and 'Snakes and

Ladders') and 're-presentation of information' ('Pollen'), which includes inferring the meaning in the problem context. 'Rope' (Figure 1.4) is another of this important type, while 'Hexcube' (Figure 1.5) is a non-routine problem in geometry, with some possible design implications. Below we shall show an 'open investigation' question, 'Consecutive Sums' (Figure 1.6, page 16), and an 'evaluation and recommendation' task, 'Crown' (Figure 1.7, page 17). Range and variety of task type is central to balancing any test.

Figure 1.5: *'Hexcube' task (for 12 to 14 year olds)*

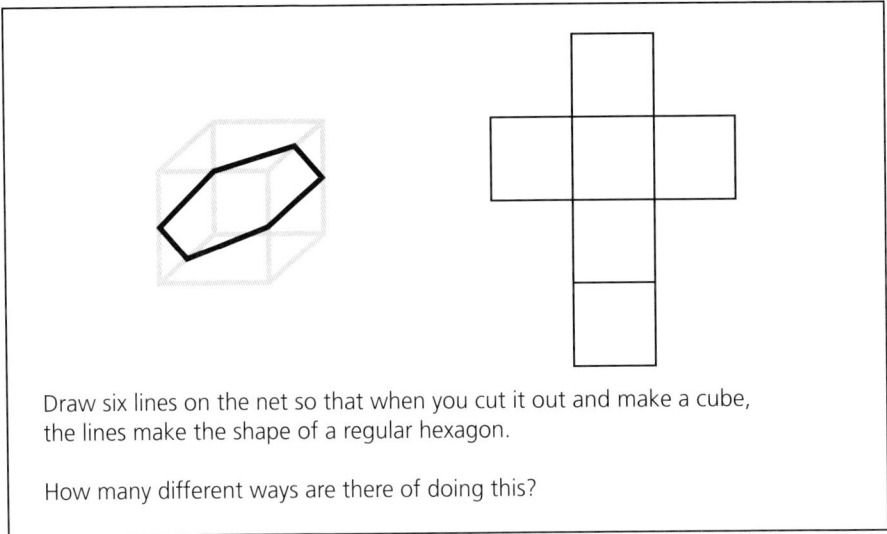

Draw six lines on the net so that when you cut it out and make a cube, the lines make the shape of a regular hexagon.

How many different ways are there of doing this?

Our draft framework for problem solving has all these dimensions, but with definitions broadened to cover those aspects of science and technology that are not much found in mathematics. I hope this brief outline brings out the constructive dialogue between the holistic and analytic viewpoints – the task set and the domain framework for balance. Both are essential but I believe that, as in most fields, the holistic should take priority. You can infer the rules of melody, harmony and counterpoint from the *Marriage of Figaro*; you cannot deduce that marvellous creation from the rules.

Finally, let me briefly mention four more principles that should not be ignored.

THE LEARNING PRINCIPLE
Assessment time should be learning time too

The traditional 'measurement' view of assessment is that it should assess what the student knows, understands and can do with as little cost as possible in time and money. It has no other function; above all, it has nothing to do with learning. As well as being false, because of WYTIWYG, this view also represents a tremendous missed opportunity. In a world where the classroom activities are not always ideal stimulants to learning, good high-stakes assessment can be a powerful *engine for improvement*. It is (unfortunately) possible that in many classrooms, some good assessment tasks will be among the most interesting and stimulating learning activities the student meets. It is certainly a worthy design ambition. Further, because they command the attention of students and teachers, they will be taken seriously.

Investigative microworlds provide an excellent genre and the computer offers a fine environment for presenting these, both in mathematics and science. 'Consecutive Sums' (Figure 1.6) is a simple but rich mathematical microworld with a host of interesting results to discover, and to explain, in open investigation. For example, you will find by exploring examples that only the powers of 2 (2, 4, 8...) cannot be expressed as sums of consecutive whole numbers. Why? This is a challenging question, but there are other interesting easier ones too.

Figure 1.6: *'Consecutive Sums' task (for 12 to 14 year olds)*

The number 15 can be written as the sum of consecutive whole numbers in exactly three different ways: 15 = 7 + 8
15 = 1 + 2 + 3 + 4 + 5
15 = 4 + 5 + 6

The number 9 can be written as the sum of consecutive whole numbers in two ways: 9 = 2 + 3 + 4
9 = 4 + 5

Look at other numbers and find out all you can about writing them as sums of consecutive whole numbers. You may want to start with the numbers from 1 to 36.
a) What patterns did you find?   b) Why do you think they occur?

THE CULTURAL VALUE PRINCIPLE
Making assessment interesting
In the assessment of language, it is taken for granted that the texts that students face should be better-than-mundane. They should have value as pieces of writing worth reading. There may be argument over which pieces are appropriate but the principle of literary value is accepted. The same cannot be said of most assessment tasks in mathematics or science. Do they embody something memorable? Do they spark interest? Rarely – they are often profoundly mundane.

'Crown' (Figure 1.7, page 17) and some of the other tasks here suggest something of what can be done.

THE RELIABILITY PRINCIPLE
Ensure accuracy of measurement
The results of assessment must have meaning, so reliability is important. I mention this briefly to show that it is not forgotten; however, it is not the main theme here. It is dangerous to make accuracy of measurement a priority. It so often leads to violating the other principles above – to measuring those things that are easy to assess, justifying it by correlation arguments. Height is well-correlated with mathematical performance over the age range five to 18. Why not just measure that?

THE DESIGN PRINCIPLE
Simplicity in use may mean sophistication in design
I hope that this needs no elaboration.

Figure 1.7: *'Crown' task (for 14 to 16 year olds)*

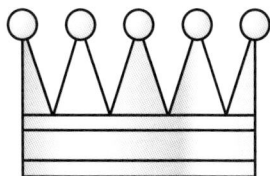

The King asks Archimedes if his crown is made from pure gold.
He knows that the crown is either pure gold or it may have some silver in it.

Archimedes works out that the volume of the crown is 140 cm³ and that its mass is 2 kilograms.

He also knows that 1 kilogram of gold has a volume of about 50 cm³ and 1 kilogram of silver has a volume of about 100 cm³

1. Is the crown pure gold? Explain how you know.

2. If the crown is not pure gold, then how much silver is in it?
   Show all your working.

Automata or thinkers?

Coming full circle, I want to return to focus on what our students need from the curriculum and its assessment. Why is problem solving so important? At one time, a person with a limited set of handwriting or calculating skills could rely on them to make a fair living; now there are very inexpensive *automata* – word processors and calculators – that perform these functions reliably. For a relatively small sum of money one can buy something that will perform automatically all the technical operations of school mathematics (graphing, statistics, algebra…). The mathematical education of a student from age five to 18 is far more costly! What is society getting for the money spent on it?

In life and work people are now asked to tackle non-routine tasks that they have *not* practised at school. If they are to be employable, they need a much wider range of higher level strategic skills – that is, problem solving skills, which include skills of reasoning, organisation and communication. The need is for flexibility, adaptability, and self-propelled learning.

People who are trained simply to be efficient *automata* are losing their jobs all over the world to real robots. The economic prosperity of any country depends on its effectiveness as a nation of *thinkers*. These are the attributes in which humans can excel; they also bring personal satisfaction. More flexible, adaptable thinkers are what a country needs. This applies particularly to those countries with a high standard of living. As Marc Tucker put it:

> *The choice for us is between a high-skill high-wage or a low-skill low-wage economy; we can't for much longer enjoy a low-skill high-wage economy. (Tucker, 2000)*

We must ask, subject-by-subject, how the different elements of curriculum and of assessment can contribute to preparing us for this change. It seems clear that gifted and talented children, who cope easily with the current curriculum, should be educated to this broader range of challenges. We hope that World Class Tests will provide both stimulus and, through the surround materials, some support for this.

There are wider implications for all children – one must surely also ask whether the ability to solve varied problems, an essential complement to skill acquisition at any level, needs more attention in both curriculum and assessment.

2 Problem solving in technology-rich environments

Randy Elliot Bennett and Hilary Persky
Educational Testing Service, Princeton, New Jersey, USA

THE PROBLEM SOLVING IN TECHNOLOGY-RICH ENVIRONMENTS (TRE) study is one of several research studies designed to lay the groundwork for incorporating new technology in the US National Assessment of Educational Progress (NAEP). NAEP is the only continuing, representative survey of what US students know and are able to do in school subjects. The TRE study has two main purposes. The first is to demonstrate one innovative use of computers in NAEP by developing *example* modules to assess problem solving with technology. The second is to answer research questions related to the measurement, equity, efficiency and operational implications of using new technology in NAEP.

These example modules will use the computer to present tasks that cannot be delivered through conventional paper-and-pencil means but which we believe tap important emerging skills. The subject-matter context for the modules will be physical science. However, it should be noted that similar measures could be built for other fields of science, for mathematics and for social science domains. The example modules sample from a universe of content domains and technology environments. We would suggest that the construct, 'Problem Solving in Technology-Rich Environments' might conceivably span biology, ecology, physics, economics and history. Similarly, we suggest that various technology-rich environments could be used in these content domains including databases, text editors, simulation tools, dynamic visual displays of information, spreadsheets, and presentation tools.

For our example modules, we chose to sample from that universe so that the *same* basic content – the science associated with gas balloons – carries through different technology environments. Table 2.1 (page 20) represents this domain conception. In the table, the TRE measure is indicated within the substantive area of physics. The measure is depicted as incorporating several technology uses (each marked by an *x*) within the same problem context. Note that this path through the domain results in an assessment very different in character from what would have occurred had we taken a horizontal path (that is, focused on a single technology use across different content domains).

For brief notes on the US education system, please see page 128.

Table 2.1: *A domain conception for problem solving in technology-rich environments*

TECHNOLOGY-RICH ENVIRONMENTS	BIOLOGY	ECOLOGY	PHYSICS *Balloon*	ECONOMICS	HISTORY
Database			X		
Text editor			X		
Simulation			X		
Dynamic visual display of information			X		
Spreadsheet			X		
Presentation and communication tools					

Guiding principles for development

Development of the TRE modules has been guided by the following principles:

- **TRE should be an assessment, not instruction, but students should be able to learn from it incidentally.** Because individual states are responsible for curriculum and because NAEP's charge by law is assessment, NAEP must be careful not to stray from its mission. However, there is no reason why NAEP should not create outstanding assessments that are also educationally worthwhile. Such assessments may, in fact, provide one potential means for building greater participation in the programme.
- **TRE should use the computer to do what can't easily be done on paper.** The TRE study will explore the measurement of skills that are becoming important because of the computer. In addition, we hope it will suggest ways in which traditional content might be measured more effectively through technology.
- **TRE should represent the type of problem solving done with computers in educational and work environments.** There are two propositions associated with this principle. The first is that problem solving in technology-rich environments is multidimensional. That is, success requires both knowledge of the substantive domain in which the problem is set and skill in using technological tools. The second proposition is that problem solving in technology-rich environments is driven by the substantive problem, not by the technology: successful problem solvers in a domain tend to look for the tool that is best suited to their problem, not a problem suited to the tool that is closest at hand.
- **TRE should be positioned so it can inform the development of a future assessment of emerging skills or of more traditional subject matter.** We are attempting to give our client, the National Center for Education Statistics, the option of employing tasks like these as part of an assessment of skill in problem solving with technology generally or as part of an existing content-based assessment like science.
- **As far as possible, TRE should allow us to disentangle component skills.** The fact that problem solving in technology-rich environments is multidimensional offers the opportunity to describe performance with something more than a single summary score. Lower levels of description may be important because what underlies an overall performance may be critical to understanding where our schools need to improve.

The target population for the TRE modules is composed of eighth grade students attending public and private schools in the United States. We assume that these students have at least basic computer skills. We believe this assumption is tenable given that the ratio of students to computers in US schools in 1999–2000 was about 5:1 (Market Data Retrieval, 2000). Because of the prevalence of experimental methodology and physics content in eighth grade science curricula, we assume that members of the population have had some basic exposure to scientific enquiry and to basic concepts of mass and volume. We also assume that they can read scientifically oriented material at a sixth grade level.

What is being measured?

Our measurement goal for the modules is to be able to judge, with some degree of certainty, level of proficiency in solving science problems presented in a technology-rich environment. We have defined that proficiency to include a combination of scientific enquiry and computer skills that might be best thought of as an 'electronic scientific-enquiry skill.' For this skill, we wish to make judgements both for the target population and for relevant sub-populations.

SCIENTIFIC-ENQUIRY SKILL

How do we define the components of this electronic scientific-enquiry skill? By *scientific enquiry skill*, we mean being able to find information about a given topic, judge what is relevant to a problem, plan and conduct experiments, monitor one's efforts, organise and interpret results, and communicate a coherent explanation. We should note that the essential features of classroom scientific enquiry are acknowledged to vary along several dimensions, with some implementations considered to be 'full' and others 'partial' enquiry (Olson and Loucks-Horsley, 2000, pp. 28–30). Our implementation is one of partial enquiry; full enquiry gives greater attention to question choice, explanation, and connections of those explanations with scientific knowledge than we are able to give in these modules. Our choice of partial enquiry is largely a practical one based on limited testing time, the need to impose constraints for assessment that would be unnecessary in an instructional context and the need to provide an example that could be taken either in the direction of a content-based assessment or a more general 'problem-solving with technology' assessment.

COMPUTER SKILL

For the second proficiency component, *computer skill*, we mean not computer skill in general, but something considerably more focused and lower level. We mean:
• being able to carry out the (mostly) *mechanical* operations of using a computer to find information, run simulated experiments, get information from dynamic visual displays, construct a table or graph, sort data and enter text; and
• being able to monitor one's efforts.

This conception is based on the belief that, in the extreme (that is, separated from all substantive knowledge), computer skill is nothing more than automatised pointing, clicking and keying. These actions become automatised through repeated practice with different software applications. We can take advantage of this fact for measurement purposes by building into our assessments the interface conventions found in common applications. Because computer-familiar students will have developed the appropriate schema, they should negotiate our assessment more quickly and effectively than their less computer-familiar counterparts. However, when we integrate this lower-level computer competency with scientific enquiry, we get a purposeful, content driven, decidedly *non*-mechanical use of the computer for scientific problem solving.

OUTCOMES

What will be reported? For the target population, as well as for relevant sub-populations, we will likely report levels of proficiency for *overall skill* in problem solving in technology-rich environments, for *scientific enquiry skill*, and for *computer skill*. In addition, we may segment scientific enquiry skill further into *exploration* (that is, carrying out the activities related to answering a given question) and *synthesis* (that is, answering the question itself). Finally, we will report a descriptive summary of key student behaviours (for example, how often students made predictions, how often they created tables and graphs).

Measurement issues

This design poses several measurement issues. First, there may be instances where a lack of one component skill interferes with measurement of the other. In one sense, this is not a serious difficulty: to solve problems successfully in a real-world technology environment, the component skills must come into play in an *integrated* manner. Arguably, it is this integration that is of ultimate interest. However, we have also stated as a development principle that the components are of interest, in part because they may help in understanding the integrated performance and its implications for improving education. The issue for the TRE design is that some students might have scientific enquiry skills or conceptual knowledge that is not up to the level of our particular substantive problem and, therefore, these students might not be able to show their technology skill at all. Similarly, there may be students whose computer skills do not meet the demands of our example and who, consequently, are unable to show their scientific enquiry skill.

A second issue is generalisability. In this study, we will collect data on how a non-representative sample of students applies a few technology tools to a small number of substantive problems. The sample will be non-representative because many schools will not have the necessary level of computer technology. Thus, we will obviously be unable to extrapolate TRE results to problem solving in technology-rich environments generally, nor to the nation's eighth graders as a whole.

Finally, there is construct validity. Typically, in such a study we would collect data from measures that were both theoretically related to and distinct from our experimental one. We would do this in an effort to locate our measure in a multidimensional space consistent with our theoretical expectations, thereby lending support to the meaning of scores. Part of that analysis involves ruling out plausible competing hypotheses for performance. Plausible competing hypotheses might include that the TRE modules are unduly influenced by reading comprehension, that they measure the same types of science skill assessed in paper and pencil, or that they are primarily a measure of general ability. For this project, we are greatly restricted in the additional measures we can administer by the limited time for which we can test students.

For the study, we will administer five measures. The first measure is a test of prior knowledge related to the science and uses of gas balloon flight. This measure is intended to give a sense of which (and how many) students have enough prior knowledge that they may come to the assessment already knowing the relationships we are asking them to discover. The second measure is a computer background questionnaire that includes a few computer skills items. This device will provide an independent indicator of computer familiarity. Thirdly, we will administer a demographic questionnaire to describe the sample and allow for sub-group comparisons. Finally, we will give two closely related TRE modules intended to measure different aspects of the complex construct described above. Both modules revolve around the science of gas balloon flight. The modules are 'Search' and 'Simulation'. The Search module asks the student to use a web-search tool to answer questions about the science and scientific uses of gas balloons. The Simulation module requires the student to use a 'what-if?' tool to uncover scientific relationships about gas balloon flight.

The TRE Simulation Module

The TRE Search and Simulation modules are being developed through a process of evidence-centred design (Mislevy, Steinberg, Breyer, Almond and Johnson, 1999a, 1999b). This focuses the developer on identifying the claims to be made on the basis of assessment results, the evidence needed to support those claims, the behaviours that will provide that evidence and the tasks required to elicit those behaviours. This structured process is particularly suited to the creation of complex assessments, which typically have high development costs. The process is intended to increase the likelihood that assessment components will be reusable and to allow for clear linkages from each test item to the claim(s) that item was intended to support. The remainder of this paper will focus on the Simulation module, as its development is nearer completion.

The TRE Simulation module asks the student to use scientific enquiry and computer skills to solve problems related to the physics of gas balloon flight. The module presents a simulation tool that students can use to answer 'what-if?' questions about balloon behaviour. The module draws on the research of Glaser and associates (Shute and Glaser, 1990, 1991; Schauble, Glaser, Raghavan, and Reiner, 1991; Raghavan, Sartoris and Glaser, 1998), as well as that of White (White and Frederiksen, 1998). The common theme running through this work is the 'discovery environment' – a microworld where a student can experiment to construct an understanding of some underlying phenomenon. Although these environments have primarily been used for instructional purposes, they also hold promise for assessment.

A second basis for our work is formed by the published standards for students' science and technology skills (for example, International Society for Techology in Education, 1998; National Committee on Science Education Standards and Assessment, 1995). These standards typically cite as key proficiencies scientific enquiry, problem solving with technology and the use of simulation. Evidence for standing on the overall 'problem solving in technology-rich environments' construct measured by the module will be drawn from what students do with the simulation tool and how effectively they answer questions about the science of gas balloon flight. Thus, we are attempting to use both product and process information to make inferences about student skill.

In the context of the Simulation module, we define *computer skill* as a subset of the definition given above, which applies to the Search and Simulation modules in combination. For the Simulation module alone, computer skill means:
- being able to carry out the mechanical operations of using a computer to run simulated experiments, get information from dynamic visual displays, construct a table or graph, sort data, and enter text; and
- being able to monitor one's efforts.

We hypothesise that students with high-level computer skills will provide the following types of evidence of their proficiency; the more positive instances that are provided, the stronger should be our belief in a high level of computer skill for that student. Students with high computer skill should:
- use the simulation tool, *regardless of substantive correctness*, to carry out the mechanics of selecting values, for: making predictions; running experiments; creating tables and/or graphs; sorting data and drawing conclusions;
- make observations about balloon behaviour based on a dynamic visual display;
- use computer HELP facility sparingly;
- respond to computer HELP appropriately.

For the Simulation module, *scientific enquiry skill* means being able to judge what information is relevant to a problem, plan and conduct experiments, monitor one's efforts, organise and interpret results, and communicate a coherent explanation. Students with high scientific enquiry skill should:
- make accurate predictions about balloon behaviour.
- pose experiments that build on previous ones by systematically controlling variables (Schauble *et al.* 1991; Shute and Glaser, 1990).
- run enough experiments (with appropriate data points) to support defensible conclusions (Schauble *et al.* 1991; Shute and Glaser, 1990).
- organise data appropriate to the problem in a table or graph.
- draw correct conclusions about the physics of balloon flight.
- respond accurately to final synthesising multiple-choice questions about the physics of balloon flight.
- use science HELP facility sparingly.
- respond to science HELP appropriately.

The above behaviours represent a hypothesis about the features that distinguish novices from proficient performers in our problem-solving domain. To test this hypothesis, however, we will need to compare the performance of students whom we already know to be novices in computer skill and in scientific enquiry skill with that of students we know to be proficient. Such a study will allow us to refine these initial claims.

PROBLEM 1

The Simulation tool interface for Problem 1 is shown in Figure 2.1 (page 25). The problem the student is to solve is in the upper right-hand corner. It asks the student to determine the relationship between mass and altitude. The interface is organised to facilitate a structured enquiry process built around designing an experiment, running it, and interpreting results. To design an experiment, the student may choose values for the independent variable (that is, mass) or make a prediction. To interpret results, he or she may construct a table, display a graph or draw conclusions.

Figure 2.1: *The Simulation tool interface*

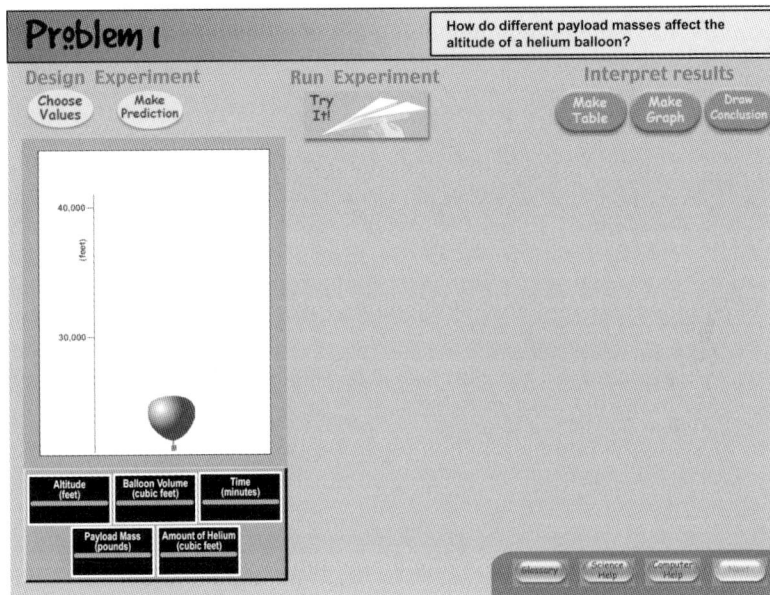

The student can attempt this process in any order and conduct as many experiments as desired. Simulation results are presented in the flight box on the left of the screen and by the instrument panel below it. Values are displayed for the altitude reached by the balloon, the volume the balloon achieves, the time taken to reach that volume and altitude, the payload mass, and the amount of helium put into the balloon (which is held constant for this problem).

Three forms of HELP are offered, as indicated by the buttons in the lower right-hand corner. These link to a glossary of science terms, science HELP and computer HELP. Computer HELP describes the functions of the simulation-tool interface. Science HELP gives hints on the substance of the problem.

A brief, animated tutorial demonstrates how to use the Simulation tool. The student can then begin working with the tool by choosing a value for mass, the independent variable. Figure 2.2 (page 26) shows the resulting screen.

Note immediately that we have imposed two constraints on the problem. First, we limit the student's choice of the independent variable to mass. Second, we fix the values of mass that the student can select. We imposed these constraints because of time limitations and concern that the problem would otherwise be too difficult for many eighth graders.

After choosing a value for the independent variable, the student might (or might not) choose to make a prediction. If he or she wants to do so, that can be achieved by pressing on the 'Make Prediction' button, which appears under 'Design Experiment'.

25

Figure 2.2: *Choosing a value for the independent variable*

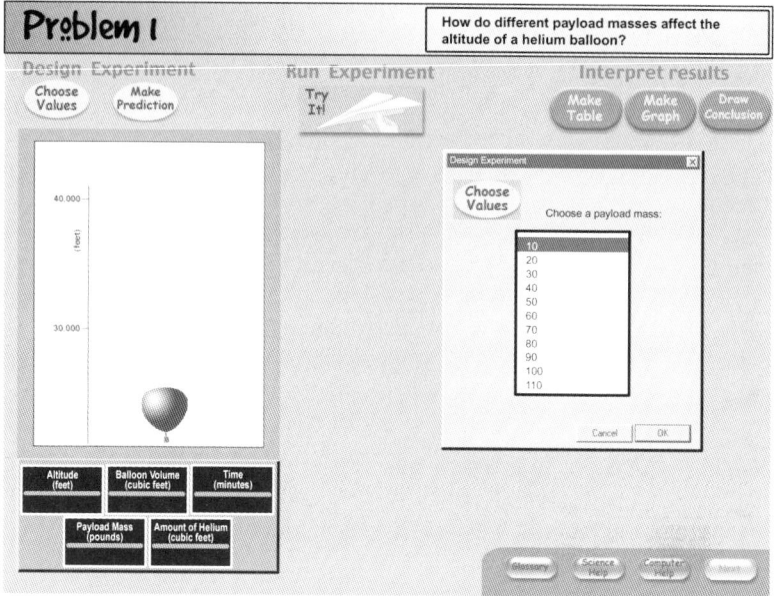

Figure 2.3: *Making a prediction*

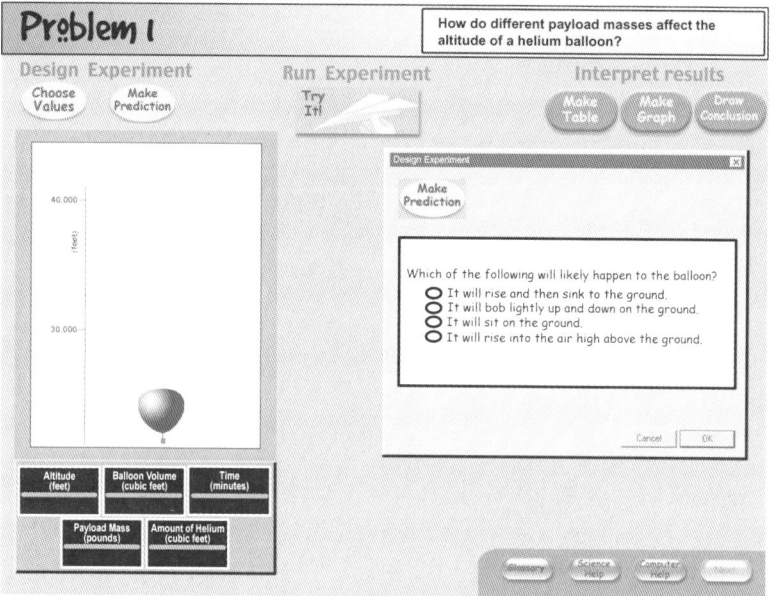

This action brings up a list of four possible outcomes (see Figure 2.3) intended to encourage the student to think about the impact on altitude of varying the balloon's mass.

When the student is ready to run an experiment, pressing 'Try It!' causes the instrument display to activate and may cause the balloon in the flight box to rise (see Figure 2.4, page 27).

Figure 2.4: *Running the experiment*

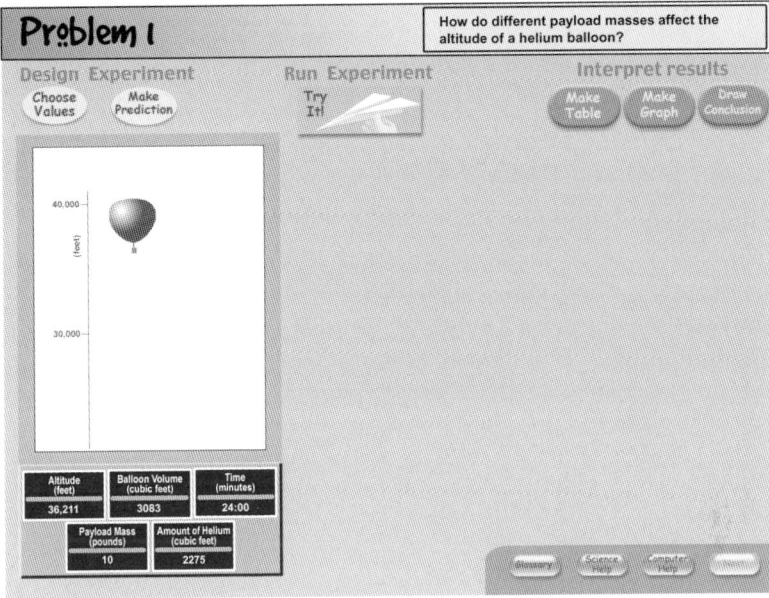

Figure 2.5: *Choosing variables for a table*

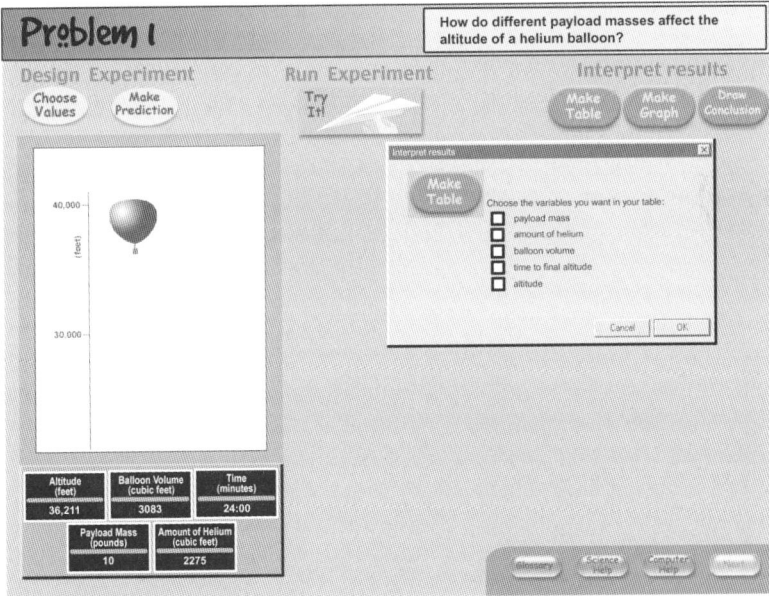

The student may decide at this point (or at any other) to interpret the results by constructing a table or graph, or by drawing a conclusion. One can make a table by pressing the appropriate button, which brings up the dialogue box shown in Figure 2.5. Note that here we allow the student leeway to get into trouble. The student constructs a table by choosing from the variables tracked in the instrument display.

The resulting table may, therefore, contain irrelevant information.

If the student chooses to include all five variables, the table will appear as in Figure 2.6. For each subsequent experiment, a line of data is added to the table automatically. The student can sort the table according to any variable by clicking on the appropriate column heading.

Figure 2.6: *A sample table*

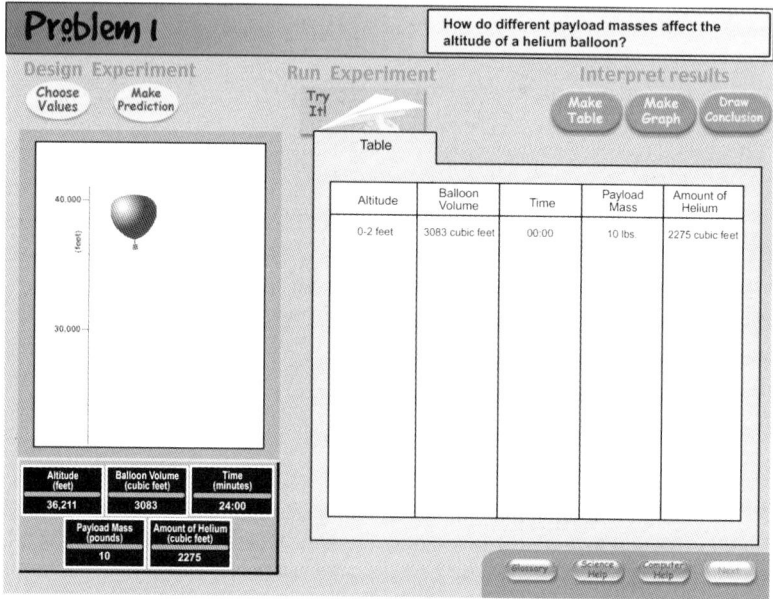

Figure 2.7: *Choosing variables for a graph*

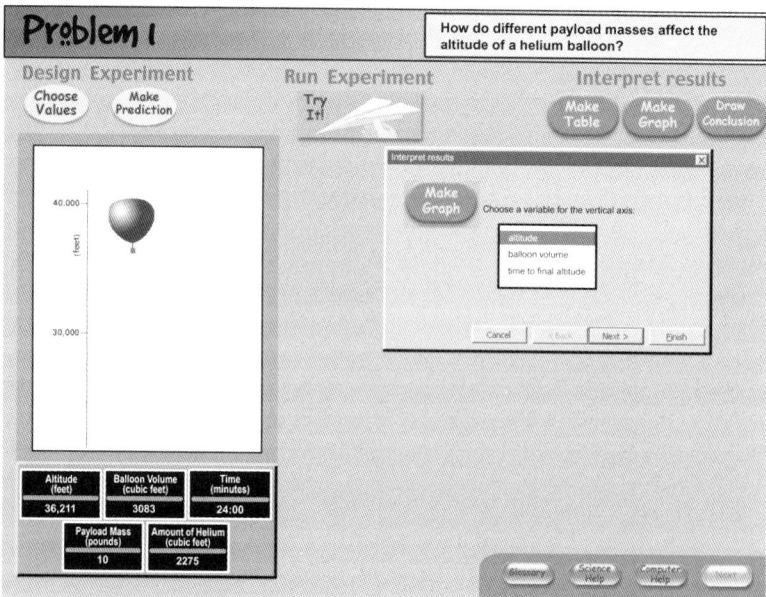

A graph can be created in a similar manner. After pressing on the 'Make Graph' button, a dialogue box appears that asks the student to select a variable for the vertical axis (see Figure 2.7) and then the horizontal axis. Again, the student is allowed to create information displays that may not be relevant.

Figure 2.7: *Choosing variables for a graph*

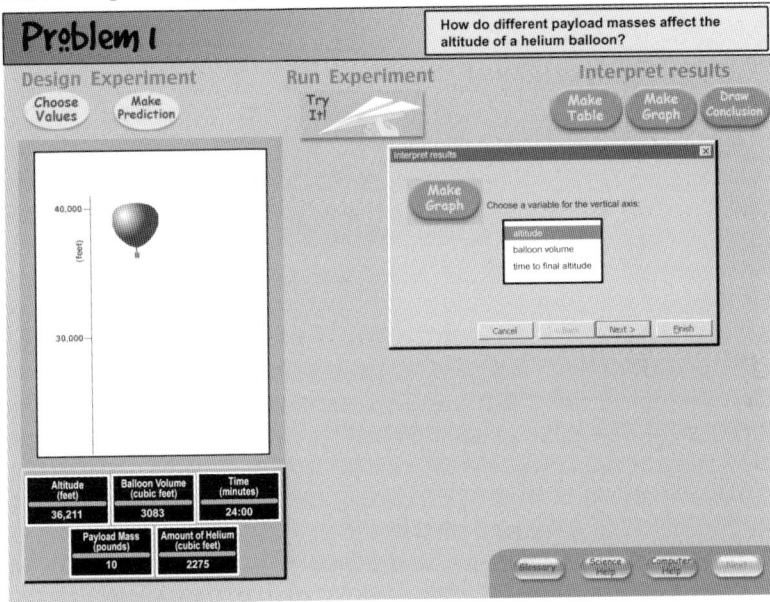

If the appropriate variables are selected, the graph should look like the one in Figure 2.8 (page 30). Note that the underlying relationship we want students to discover is a simple negative linear one: as mass increases, the altitude the balloon can achieve decreases. Note also that, in the absence of any knowledge of the form of the underlying mass–altitude relationship, we would expect the proficient student to choose carefully the number and spread of values for mass. Too few values or too narrow a range would fail to confirm that the underlying relationship is linear throughout.

The last action the student may wish to take is to draw a conclusion. Pressing this button brings up a text-entry box (see Figure 2.9, page 30). This box calls for an answer to the question about how payload mass affects altitude and asks that the answer be supported with experimental observations. Before finishing the conclusion, the student may choose to revisit an existing table or graph, construct new tables or graphs, or conduct more experiments. Following this screen, we may pose related questions that students can answer by choosing from a key-list. These questions could provide a more accurate measure for students who are unable to express themselves in free-form writing.

This initial problem is followed by two additional ones. The first of these asks the student to discover a more complex, bivariate, non-linear relationship. The second asks the student to discover how two independent variables work together to determine a third quantity.

Figure 2.8: *A sample graph*

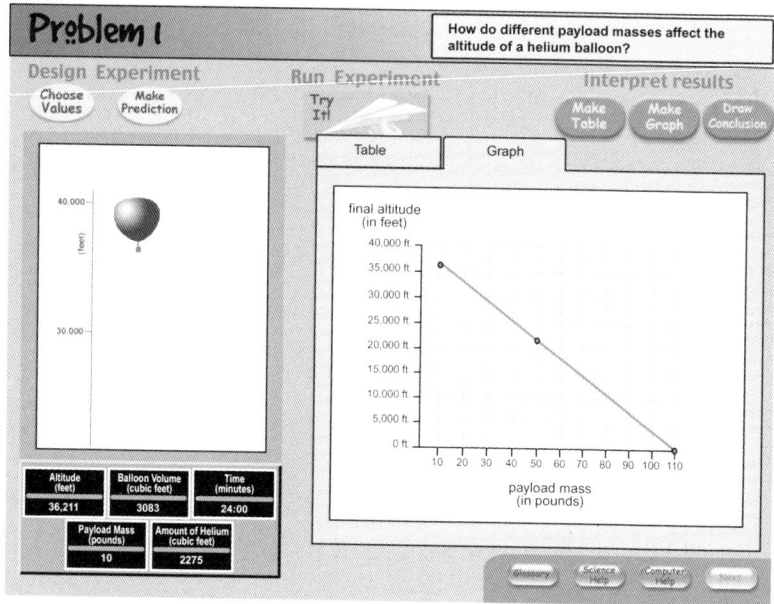

Figure 2.9: *Drawing a conclusion*

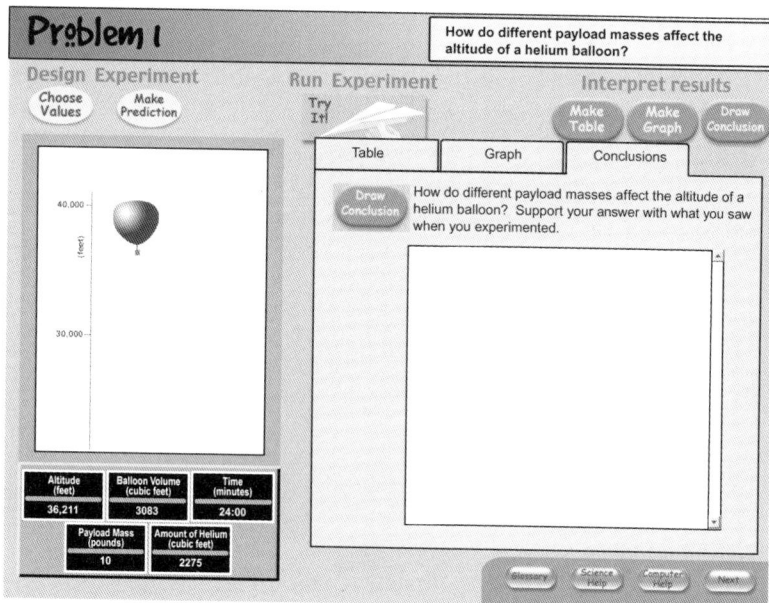

SCORING

At the time of writing, our specifications for scoring are not complete, though the general outline is clear. We expect scoring to be a three-step process of feature extraction, feature evaluation, and evidence aggregation. The first step, feature extraction, will entail deciding what elements of a student response to isolate from the complete transaction record for scoring purposes. To identify those elements, we will work from the behaviours we expect proficient performers to display.

The second step, feature evaluation, will involve assigning a score to each extraction. Dichotomous scoring will be appropriate for some extractions, whereas others may be amenable to partial-credit schemes. For example, we might award one point for every correct prediction that the student makes. At the same time, we might decide to score students' written conclusions for each of the problems on a four-point scale. Feature evaluations will be done automatically where feasible.

The final step, evidence aggregation, entails combining the feature scores in a principled manner that allows us to connect student behaviours to inferences about performance. Because we are interested in capturing the multi-dimensionality inherent in these modules, we are planning to do this aggregation using inference networks, which offer a formal statistical framework for reasoning about interdependent variables in the presence of uncertainty. (See Mislevy, Almond, Yan and Steinberg, 1999, for technical details on using these networks in educational testing.)

As part of this approach, we will depict our theory about what is being measured by TRE as a *student model*. This model organises the components of proficiency in the domain of problem solving in technology-rich environments. That organisation falls directly out of the discussion above, which posits that problem solving in technology-rich environments is composed of computer skill and scientific enquiry skill. These skills may, in turn, be comprised of further elements; for example, exploration and synthesis represent a possible decomposition of scientific enquiry.

Standing on each student model variable is expressed in terms of a proficiency level with some degree of uncertainty. Any number of levels may be assigned, but for our purposes three levels might be sufficient. Those levels might be termed, 'proficient', 'intermediate' and 'novice'. Our uncertainty regarding a student's standing takes the form of the probability that he or she is at each level.

Each of the observations we make is connected to one or more variables in the student model. The connections determine the likelihood of observing a particular feature evaluation (for example, a written conclusion receiving four points) given a particular configuration of the student model (for example, proficient on all skills). These probabilities may initially be set subjectively or on the basis of available information. As data are collected, the probabilities (and the model itself) can be refined.

When a student takes a module, the score for each feature is used to update our belief about the student's standing on the skill component to which the feature is connected. Thus, observing a score of 4 for one of the Simulation conclusions would increase our belief (that is, probability) in that student being proficient in synthesis skill. This increase would then propagate to other skills linked to synthesis. So, the probability that the student was proficient in scientific enquiry would also increase, as would that for problem solving in technology-rich environments. This updating of the student model is carried out until all feature evaluations are incorporated. We can then generate a profile that gives the proficiency level for each model variable, and the uncertainty associated with that level, for individuals, sub-groups and the test population.

The Relationship between the Simulation and Search modules

Whether the Simulation module should be employed in conjunction with the Search module is unresolved. On the one hand, it is widely recognised that successful problem solving requires content knowledge in addition to domain-dependent and domain independent strategies (Baker and O'Neil, in press). Similarly, current conceptions of scientific enquiry stress the integration of content knowledge with scientific process (Olson and Loucks-Horsley, 2000). These conceptions would argue for presenting Simulation and Search in combination, using one to help with the other. That is, one might imagine students using Search to develop their knowledge of mass, volume, and gas balloons as they are attempting to solve the problems presented in Simulation. Similarly, one could conceivably answer a question posed in Search with both information gained from the web and experimental results generated through Simulation.

Whereas combined use is theoretically attractive, it poses practical problems. Most critically, combined use might require more student time than participating schools would be willing to offer. Even if that time could be made available, it might have to be distributed across more than one testing session, increasing administration costs and potentially allowing student performance to be influenced by other sources.

Potential uses in NAEP

How might assessments like TRE be used in NAEP? One potential use is as a survey measure of problem solving with technology. Following development of a framework for this domain, which would be created by the National Assessment Governing Board, one would generate several TRE modules, each with different substantive problems. These modules might be designed to cross substantive problems and technology use (that is, several types of computer use in each of several problem contexts). Each of these modules would then be randomly assigned to a different group of students, with some students taking more than one module to allow for estimating covariances among the modules. One would then estimate population performance on the full set of modules from the performance of the samples taking each one.

Another use would be as part of a 'multiple-methods' NAEP (Pellegrino, Jones and Mitchell, 1999) conducted within an existing content framework (for example, science, history or mathematics). In this conception, conventional paper-and-pencil survey tests would be employed to sample the content domain broadly. In addition, extended computer-delivered tasks would be used with smaller samples to provide a deeper, more qualitative understanding of what students can do in segments of the domain that cannot be probed as deeply with standard methods.

Conclusion

The TRE project is being conducted as one of several studies that will lay the groundwork for incorporating new technology in NAEP. TRE is intended to demonstrate one innovative use of computers in NAEP by developing an example set of modules to assess problem solving with technology. This paper has described one of those modules, Simulation, in detail.

We can perhaps best summarise the essence of the TRE study by reiterating its development principles and how the project has attempted to realise them:

- **TRE should be an assessment, not instruction, but students should be able to learn from it incidentally.** We believe that the evidence-centered design approach used to create TRE has put us in good position to make targeted inferences from performance about student skills. We also believe that most students will find working with the assessment to be more of a learning experience than the typical large-scale test provides.

- **TRE should use the computer to do what can't easily be done on paper.** The TRE modules allow students to explore 'what-if?' questions, interpret a dynamic visual display, and use electronic information search. In addition, the modules allow us to track the processes students use in problem-solving. None of these capabilities could be easily achieved with conventional testing technology.

- **TRE should represent the type of problem solving done with computers in educational and work environments.** TRE attempts to capture the multi-dimensionality characteristic of problem solving by requiring students to demonstrate both basic facility with the computer and substantive skill. We have tried to emphasise technology as a means, rather than an end, by carrying the same problem context across different technology uses.

- **TRE should be positioned so it can inform the development of a future assessment of emerging skills or of more traditional subject matter.** It should be possible to incorporate meaningful exercises built around using a simulation tool or electronic information search into existing NAEP subject-matter assessments. It should also be possible to use the TRE modules as initial models for measures of problem solving with technology generally.

- **As far as possible, TRE should allow us to disentangle component skills.** To assist students with low science skills, we demonstrate enquiry in the Simulation tutorial, organise the interface to encourage good enquiry, include a glossary of science terms, progressively stage problem difficulty, and provide science HELP. For those students with low computer skills, we demonstrate how to use the interface in the tutorial, use familiar interface conventions (like the dialogue boxes found in most Windows software), and provide computer HELP. Third, as part of the assessment we collect evidence relevant to each of the specific component skills. Finally, we are using a measurement model capable of handling the multi-dimensionality inherent in this type of assessment.

This work was done under co-operative agreement for the Office of Educational Research and Improvement, National Center for Education Statistics, Washington, DC 20208, CFDA#84.902F. The positions expressed herein do not necessarily represent those of OERI or of Educational Testing Service.

3 The Rich Task: a new assessment species for new times

Gabrielle Matters

New Basics Branch, Education Queensland, Australia

THIS IS THE STORY OF A NEW ASSESSMENT AND REPORTING REGIME being trialled in government schools in Queensland, Australia. Delivery of education in these government schools, all of which are co-educational, is the responsibility of Education Queensland. Approximately 76 per cent of primary school students and 64 per cent of secondary school students attend government schools but there is an ongoing drift to the non-government sector.

Queensland is the only State in Australia where the population of the capital city (Brisbane) is less than the population outside it. In the 2001 State election, the Labour Government was returned with an increased majority. One of its election commitments had been the expansion of the New Basics Project (see Education Queensland, 2000a or visit http://www.education.qld.gov.au/corporate/newbasics) – the source of the Rich Tasks that are the topic of this chapter.

The Rich Task (RT) is a reconceptualisation of the notion of *outcome* as demonstration of mastery; that is, students display their understandings, knowledges and skills through performance on transdisciplinary activities that have an obvious connection to the wide world. These activities draw upon skills across disciplines while retaining the integrity of each disciplinary methodology. Their approach is not the same as that of the traditional 'interdisciplinary' activities, which seek thematic links between disciplines.

RTs are the assessable and reportable outcomes of a curriculum plan that prepares students for the challenges of 'new times' – a term coined to describe the combined phenomena of globalisation, the shift towards local and service-based economies, changing technologies, complex transformations in cultural and social relationships, fluid demographics and a sense of uncertainty about the future.

There is a strong programmatic emphasis on assessment – the moderation of teacher judgements and state-wide standards of performance to deal with the potential for 'dumbing down' (cf. McGaw, 1996) in classrooms. Reporting on RT outcomes is to provide the most elaborate portrait of student achievement over nine years of schooling ever attempted in Australia.

For brief notes on the Australian education system, please see page 129.

Of particular interest to the gifted and talented sector is the quirky nature of these tasks. Each represents a synthesis of intellectual activities – a product ideally suited to the needs and talents of bright students. The best RTs truly reflect intellectual development and are associated with assessment criteria that reward the unique qualities of student performance rather than encourage dreary predictability.

This chapter gives a conceptual overview of RTs and the dissection of one 'real' task as an example. It also includes an analysis of the task specifications and a description of how the essentials of a metaconstruct surfaced.

Background

THE NEW BASICS FRAMEWORK

The RT is one component of an integrated framework for curriculum, pedagogy and assessment. Within the New Basics Framework, the RTs are conceptualised as part of a triad. The other components are:

• the New Basics (four curriculum organisers entitled: Life pathways and social futures, Multiliteracies and communications media, Active citizenship, and Environments and technologies);
• Productive Pedagogies (20 teaching strategies – see School Reform Longitudinal Study, 1999a, 1999b).

Figure 3.1 shows the network of reciprocal relationships that exist within the triad. The New Basics are not deliverable without significant shifts in pedagogy. The New Basics and Productive Pedagogies necessitate rich and authentic assessment. The RTs exemplify and drive key elements of the new approaches.

Figure 3.1: *Conceptual pivots for the New Basics Framework*

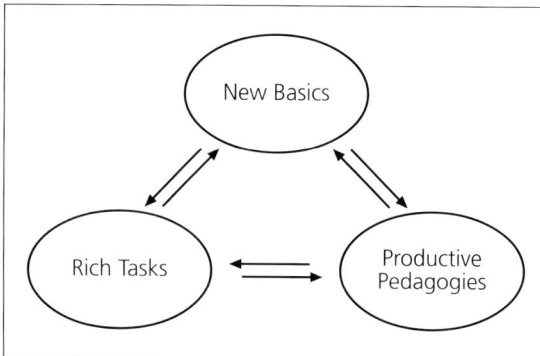

This framework attempts to empower teachers, unclutter the curriculum, 'up the ante' intellectually, deliver fewer alienated students (Education Queensland, 2000b), prepare students for an uncertain world and position the classroom in the global village. The New Basics approach focuses on students developing critical thinking, problem-solving and lifelong learning skills and applying them to real-life activities. Teachers are required to review their teaching practices and organise student activities and assessment around RTs

SETTING THE SCENE

The Queensland senior secondary system (Years 11 and 12) has externally moderated school-based assessment and standardised cross-curriculum testing (see Queensland Board of Senior Secondary School Studies, 1996); stringent quality assurance procedures accompany curriculum and assessment. The junior secondary system (Years 8 to 10) has unmoderated school-based assessment and many educationists and researchers have recommended change (Smith, Matters, Cosier and Watson, 1999; Pitman, 2000).

In the primary school, there is no mandatory assessment beyond the national literacy and numeracy testing programme – standardised tests with results reported against national benchmarks in Years 3, 5 and 7 (see Queensland School Curriculum Council, 1997). Testing regimes of this scope and dimension yield useful data but miss more than they capture. Neither do they provide insights into the varied achievements of bright students across disciplines.

A fresh approach to illuminating complex learning outcomes through evidence-based assessment is overdue in primary schooling – particularly in relation to the gifted. RTs meet these criteria and, by sharp focus and definition of boundaries, lend themselves to standard moderation procedures to ensure state-wide comparability.

In primary and lower secondary schools, then, assessment is at the crossroads. The choice for policy-makers is between a plethora of standardised tests and authentic performance-based assessment. Performance-based assessment is not new; what is new is the notion of attaching hard-edged accountabilities to it as in the New Basics Framework.

The aim of the New Basics is to teach students how to locate and evaluate critically the knowledge and skills they need in a particular situation. Assessment is viewed as a central part of the message system – not an afterthought or bolt-on to the curriculum. Neither is there any attempt to mystify or conceal the criteria for assessment. The framework treats assessment as transparent, feeding back into and enhancing curriculum and pedagogy. In this way, assessment is not only a form of accountability: its processes and products are also accountable to teachers, communities and students in a clear, comprehensible way (Myford, 1999).

The Rich Tasks model

RATIONALE

In developing this framework, Allan Luke's team (Education Queensland, 2000a) took the best ideas of the last 20 years and reinvented them with a futures orientation. The notion of RTs is based on:
- Dewey's concept of 'enterprise' and 'project' as unifying devices for the curriculum;
- Vygotsky's concept of classroom as 'zone of proximal development';
- Freire's concept of 'problem-posing' and 'problem-solving' education to teach students how to analyse and act;
- Sizer's concept of 'demonstrations of mastery' as a way to focus pedagogy and accountability in school renewal.

The first imperative of school reform, according to Sizer (1992), is to give teachers and students focus and room for intellectually rich activities. These activities are at the centre of what Sizer calls 'mindful schools'. They become a focus for pedagogy and curriculum, a means of accountability and a celebration of the intellectual life of the school. Sizer argues that the doing of these RTs provides a stronger basis for accountability to parents, stakeholders and other teachers than is possible from standardised tests or examinations. The demonstration of the tasks may engage the whole school community in their planning and presentation. The result, he argues, is crucial: instead of an enforced accountability agenda that students and teachers feel is imposed, the demonstration model provides public confirmation of mastery of important knowledge and skills for all involved in the tasks.

The Queensland model of RTs is not a call for integrated, holistic teaching. It is a call for a rigorous intellectual focus for student work that cuts through a crowded and potentially diffuse curriculum. An RT is a culminating performance that is purposeful and models real life. It presents real substantive problems to solve and engages learners in forms of pragmatic social action that have genuine value: each task demands that students engage with solving problems of significance and relevance to their community, school or region. The problems require identification, analysis and resolution and require that students analyse, theorise and intellectually engage with the wider world. Research (SRLS, 1999a, 1999b) identifies intellectual engagement and relevant work as two necessities for improved outcomes.

As well as having a real-life slant, these tasks also represent an outcome of substantial intellectual and educational value. And, to be truly rich, a task must be transdisciplinary. RTs have relevance and power in the new worlds of work and everyday life. It is important that they have recognisable face validity with educators, parents and community stakeholders. Finally, it is crucial that tasks be rich in developmental, cognitive and intellectual depth and breadth to guide curriculum planning across a significant span of schooling.

This is not a progressivist educational agenda. The delivery of a new set of basic educational outcomes for students has to be accompanied by a strong emphasis on rigour, accountability, teacher knowledge and expertise. The best performances and exhibitions are not theme-based projects aimed at motivating students; they are complex activities that evoke fundamental questions.

RANGE

For 2001–03 and 2002–04, there are 20 RTs in total (see Table 3.1). The last group of tasks spans Years 7 to 9 and is deliberately set across the primary–secondary divide to encourage dialogue between sectors. Various forms of evidence of student achievement are to be gathered and students will have the opportunity to exhibit their valuable expertise before family and community. Time allocated to RTs is estimated to be 40 to 60 per cent of class time. Reporting on student achievement occurs at the end of Years 3, 6 and 9.

Successful task completion is indicative of the student having acquired the knowledge and skills to find answers (at the requisite levels) to the following four questions:

• Who am I and where am I going?
• How do I make sense of and communicate with the world?
• What are my responsibilities in communities, cultures and economies?
• How do I describe, analyse and shape the world around me?

Table 3.1: *Set of 20 Rich Tasks*

Suite for Years 1 to 3	Suite for Years 4 to 6	Suite for Years 7 to 9
Year 3 students will . . .	Year 6 students will...	Year 9 students will...
1. WEB PAGE DESIGN...collect information about themselves, their school and their community...use this information to design web pages and respond to questions electronically.	**1. TRAVEL ITINERARIES...**design alternative itineraries of interest to a party comprising the student and an exchange student, and...an adult... identify...transport options, tourist attractions, and sites of...cultural significance...present costings and reasons for their choices.	**1. SCIENCE AND ETHICS CONFER...**explore...a biotechnological process to which there are ethical dimensions... identify scientific techniques...research...principles for coming to terms with an...ethical issue...prepare pre-conference materials for...conference...
2. MULTIMEDIA PRESENTATION ON AN ENDANGERED PLANT OR ANIMAL...investigate a threatened Australian plant or animal and the extent to which it is at risk... create a persuasive...multimedia presentation.	**2. CRITICAL REVIEW OF NARRATIVE TEXTS...**examine books written for emergent readers...select one category for further examination...present a review of a book...choose an aspect of nature... create an illustrated storybook.	**2. IMPROVING WELLBEING IN THE COMMUNITY...** work with a local community to develop a plan for improving...that local community and then enact the plan...evaluate the level of success...recommend future actions.
3. PHYSICAL FITNESS...memorise, rehearse and master dances of different forms... prepare introductions for their performed dances by investigating the role of dance and the cultural context of their dances. They will measure and monitor their fitness as they engage in a high level of physical activity.	**3. PERSONAL HEALTH PROGRAM...** identify and understand an aspect of their personal health and fitness... develop and implement a plan for improving this...By collecting, organising and presenting data... evaluate the extent to which the goals have been achieved and the contribution of factors to this improvement.	**3. THE BUILT ENVIRONMENT: DESIGNING A STRUCTURE...**identify a client's needs and take these...into account in preparing a design brief ...design an environmentally sensitive and aesthetic structure...communicate ...design through sketches, plans and models...give...consideration to structure, materials...costs.
4. READ AND TALK ABOUT STORIES...view, read and listen to fiction stories presented in different media forms...analyse characters and settings and compare... different stories and...media...present their ideas in a performance...	**4. A CELEBRATORY, FESTIVE OR ARTISTIC EVENT OR PERFORMANCE...**work within teams, in different capacities, in planning, organising, creating and performing in a celebratory, festive or artistic event or performance.	**4. AUSTRALIAN NATIONAL IDENTITY: INFLUENCES AND PERSPECTIVES...** demonstrate...understanding of... different influences...on 'Australian national identity'...through the... production...of a...filmed documentary.
5. HISTORICAL AND SOCIAL ASPECTS OF A CRAFT...explore craft as a personal, social and cultural endeavour...prepare and run a stall that showcases a chosen craft and an object or objet d'art that they have made as an example of that craft.	**5. ORAL HISTORIES AND DIVERSE AND CHANGING LIFESTYLES...** explore change in...twentieth century lifestyles, with particular reference to...work, by recording oral histories... as the basis for a finessed electronic media presentation that portrays significant changes...and predicts...change in the...future.	**5. PERSONAL CAREER DEVELOPMENT PLAN...** undertake a career planning process... describe features of a range of work options and their associated expectations; assess their...strengths, interests, achievements and areas to be developed; identify potential careers...produce an individual career development plan, including a...résumé.
	6. DESIGN, MAKE AND DISPLAY A PRODUCT...design a...product, and make the product or a working model...As part of a public display... flesh out a...marketing plan... explore ...suitability...for mass manufacture.	**6. OPINION-MAKING ORACY...**make forceful speeches on an issue of international or national significance to three unlike audiences in different forums.
	7. SPACE FUTURES...engage with the exploration of space and apply the techniques of the mathematical and physical sciences to produce a coherent experimental design, a model of the solar system...investigate the impact of space travel on life on Earth.	**7. PI IN THE SKY...**demonstrate... understanding of different mathematical approaches used to frame and answer questions about astronomy...immerse themselves in one such question and how that culture used...mathematics to frame and answer that question...present ...lessons...to communicate...essential ideas and techniques of the mathematics of the situation.
		8. INTERNATIONAL TRADE...based on knowledge of the way in which international trade occurs, and on knowledge of the needs and wants of another culture, students will identify and provide a detailed analysis of an export opportunity. They will [use] skills in a language other than English to present a talk and...literature to promote this export opportunity.

39

DIAGRAMMATIC REPRESENTATION

Figure 3.2 (opposite) shows one of the eight tasks for students in Years 7 to 9, and serves as an exemplar. Each of the 20 tasks is presented in detail thus:
• Task specs (specifications) appear as an annotated and embellished flowchart.
• The flowchart is complemented by a written synopsis of the task. This task description appears in the upper centre of the flowchart under the task identifier.

Additional text (not reproduced in Figure 3.2) provides:
• the New Basics referents;
• the targeted repertoires of practice (and operational fields of knowledge);
• ideas showing how the task might be woven into the curriculum plan;
• the task parameters, in order to clarify and enrich the RT's function as both an assessment strategy and an educational device.

The use of a flowchart for the task specs reinforces the notion that an RT is multifaceted (engaging the student in a variety of activities), sequential and integrated (some aspects of the task must be done before others, and consideration must be given to what else has or has not yet been done).

Active verbs are used to describe the task, to highlight the focused activity that it involves. A dotted frame around a description indicates that, while this aspect of the task will need to be done (and evidence to this effect might need to be collected), students are not required to demonstrate the *extent* of their achievement on it. A continuous frame around a description indicates that student achievement on this aspect is to be demonstrated and will be assessed.

It follows that the assessable facets of an RT are the set of such directly assessed demonstrations. (Trade-offs across facets will be taken account of in the overall grade – allowing higher than demanded performance in one aspect to compensate for lower performance in another.)

It is vital that teachers and students alike are made aware in advance of what constitutes high-quality performance on an RT. The assessable outcomes will be graded in terms of qualities that are communicated in a variety of ways:
• embedded in the task descriptions themselves;
• explained in the frame annotations – the brief summary of high-level performance;
• communicated in the relationship pointers – the arrows that link frames;
• implied, in that they are performance qualities known to be valued within the targeted repertoires of practice (these are the operative outcomes).

The relative sizes of the continuous frames and the extent to which they are placed in the foreground indicate the relative contribution that each facet of performance makes to a student's overall grade. A grade is the code for reporting student performance on the RT. The grades will come from moderated teacher judgements against what is known to be valued. Prompts ('clouds') indicate the values that underpin that activity, telling students what things have to be kept in mind. These might point to information sources, suggest parallel activities, explain terms used in the task specs, provide insight into high-level performance or suggest strategies for developing a certain repertoire of practice.

Task parameters are specified in order to maintain the match between task and

Figure 3.2: *Example of a Rich Task – Year 9 Rich Task no.1*

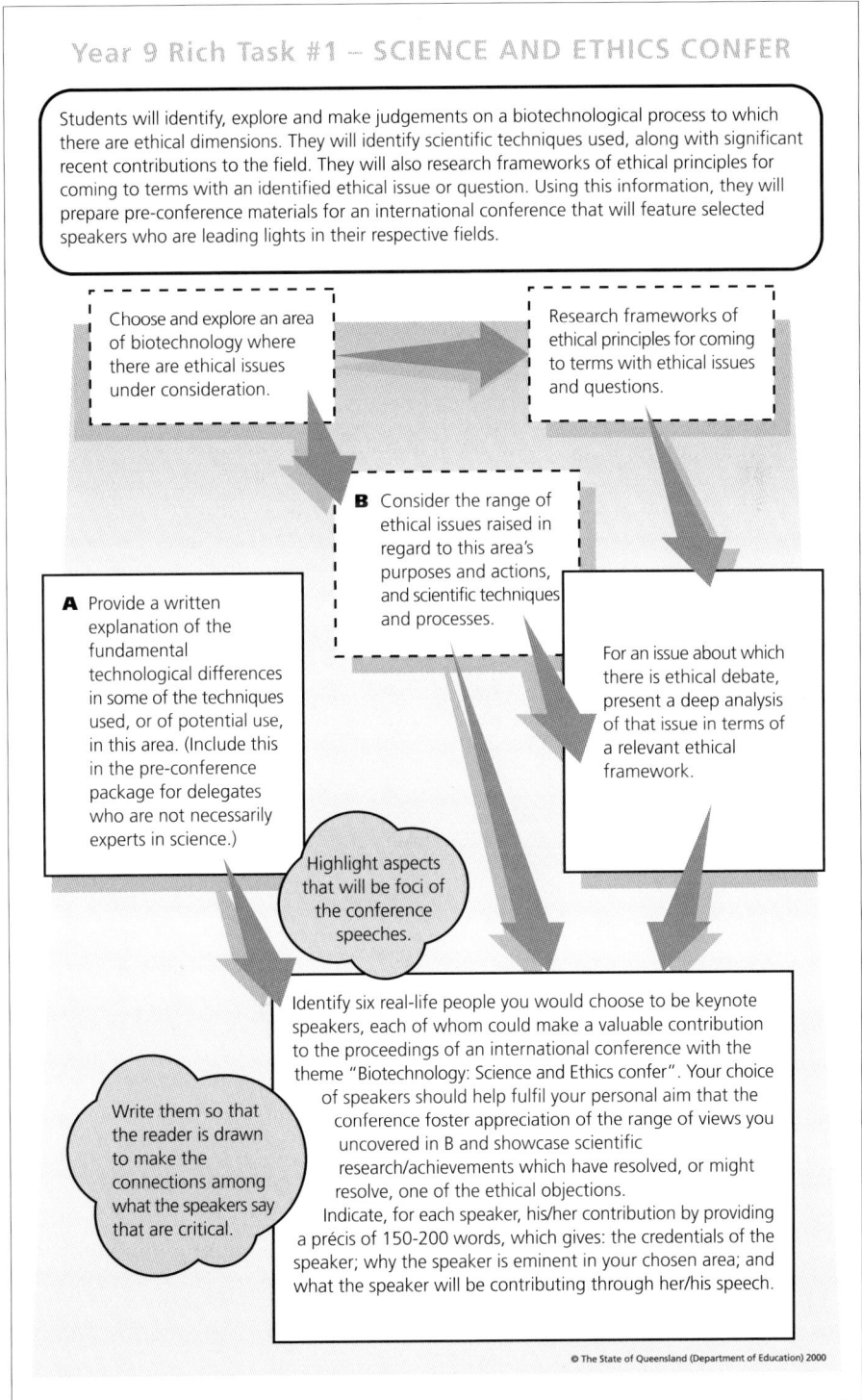

Year 9 Rich Task #1 – SCIENCE AND ETHICS CONFER

Students will identify, explore and make judgements on a biotechnological process to which there are ethical dimensions. They will identify scientific techniques used, along with significant recent contributions to the field. They will also research frameworks of ethical principles for coming to terms with an identified ethical issue or question. Using this information, they will prepare pre-conference materials for an international conference that will feature selected speakers who are leading lights in their respective fields.

Choose and explore an area of biotechnology where there are ethical issues under consideration.

Research frameworks of ethical principles for coming to terms with ethical issues and questions.

B Consider the range of ethical issues raised in regard to this area's purposes and actions, and scientific techniques and processes.

A Provide a written explanation of the fundamental technological differences in some of the techniques used, or of potential use, in this area. (Include this in the pre-conference package for delegates who are not necessarily experts in science.)

For an issue about which there is ethical debate, present a deep analysis of that issue in terms of a relevant ethical framework.

Highlight aspects that will be foci of the conference speeches.

Write them so that the reader is drawn to make the connections among what the speakers say that are critical.

Identify six real-life people you would choose to be keynote speakers, each of whom could make a valuable contribution to the proceedings of an international conference with the theme "Biotechnology: Science and Ethics confer". Your choice of speakers should help fulfil your personal aim that the conference foster appreciation of the range of views you uncovered in B and showcase scientific research/achievements which have resolved, or might resolve, one of the ethical objections.
Indicate, for each speaker, his/her contribution by providing a précis of 150-200 words, which gives: the credentials of the speaker; why the speaker is eminent in your chosen area; and what the speaker will be contributing through her/his speech.

© The State of Queensland (Department of Education) 2000

targeted repertoires of practice and operational fields. They also encourage efficient and focused demonstration of student outcomes and ensure that, across a suite of tasks, students have a range of ways in which they can demonstrate their achievement. Finally, the parameters acknowledge that teachers in different schools need a shared understanding of each task so that they have a common basis for channelling students' efforts and assessing their work.

The nature of the parameters depends on the nature of the task. If necessary, for example, they indicate whether certain aspects of the tasks are to be carried out individually or in groups, in a controlled assessment space or not, with or without certain levels of teacher assistance, and so on. The parameters also make clear any other requirements, such as the means for teachers to validate that certain activities have been carried out. For example, it may be that a diary is to be kept of individual contributions to a group task.

Tasks differ in the number of available grades for assessment and reporting because this is more than just an indicator of task complexity. It takes into account, for example, the prime intentions of the task, the task parameters and the degree to which differences in achievement can be recognised or are worth recording.

The task intensity is given in the belief that some tasks will require more effort, concentration, rigour, knowledge or skill than others. Often, this will result in an increase in the time taken to complete the task. Teachers' estimates of its duration may or may not incorporate the time for explicit teaching of essential skills and concepts before the task is carried out. In estimating time required, teachers are encouraged to take into account that the tasks are designed for efficient and focused demonstrations of what students have achieved. The tasks vary in the amount of work involved, and the time spent on a task should not be so long that students (or teachers) lose direction.

THE TEACHER'S ROLE

The tasks make explicit the sorts of activities in which students have to engage and are publicly accessible statements about the kinds of learnings that schools transmit. They invite teachers to use imagination and expertise, to work collaboratively in transdisciplinary teams in designing learning experiences. This suggests that teachers 'work backwards' from whole, educationally meaningful, valuable tasks and, using their professional judgement, break these tasks down around 'targeted repertoires' of practice.

Targeted repertoires are those skills – cognitive, cultural, linguistic and social – that students need to acquire developmentally in order to complete the task. Repertoires are expressed as clusters of genres, skills and competences; that is, gathering, doing and producing, by working individually or in teams. A study of the complete list of targeted repertoires of practice (Table 3.2) will reveal that a premium is placed on the collection, analysis and presentation of data, the presentation of self, and the 'multiliteracies' (Cazden *et al.*, 1996).

For schools to deliver, it is obvious that structural choices are required. Cautionary notes are provided concerning the practicalities of school organisation (Education Queensland, 2000a). Schools will have to orchestrate assessment 'windows' if teachers are to avoid disorganised assessment 'traffic' or intensification of workload. Because moderation of teacher judgements is to occur after assessment

Table 3.2: *Repertoires of practice to date (complete list still being developed)*

Years 1 to 3	Years 4 to 6	Years 7 to 9	
Analysing and deciding	Analysing and synthesising information, and influencing opinion based on a evaluation of that information	Applying inter-cultural understanding	Persuading through writing in both English and another language (without distortion of factual accuracy)
Appreciating and speaking about different forms of cultural expression		Applying mathematical techniques and procedures related to measurement, estimation, scale drawing, costing	**Précis writing with a purpose**
Appreciating the personal, cultural and social significance of craft and objets d'art	Applying a theoretical model to a real situation (in this case, the marketing of the product)		Presenting complex ideas textually and graphically (e.g flowcharts and timelines)
Appropriate communication strategies for audience and context	Being adept at the use of computer software such as Excel	Collecting and presenting data on clients' needs	Presenting material sequenced so as to develop an audience's mathematical knowledge, concepts, techniques, applications and sensitivities
Classifying	Collecting, recording and presenting data	Communicating and negotiating	
Collecting and collating information	Creating works to be performed for a particular purpose	Developing and implementing action plans	Project management; for example, analysing, planning, consulting, utilising human and other resources, working within government policies and frameworks
Communicating by means of an exhibition		**Etiquette of formal correspondence and protocols of introduction**	
Comparing, contrasting and relating	Designing and analysing scientific experiments, with consideration of the factors that vary and what is controlled	Evaluating and problem solving	Reading and interpreting economic data
Composing (e.g. layout, use of colour, images)		Facility in financial mathematics (including exchange rates)	Report writing
Comprehending the concepts of ecological interrelatedness and environmental responsibility	Evaluating on the basis of data	Film-making, particularly making documentaries: from creative production to polished presentation	Researching and interviewing
Conceiving, designing and executing	Exploiting sound/music/silences, and possibly visual images, in order to illustrate the selected excerpts of oral histories, to create/sustain/change mood, tone and so on, and to contribute to unity		Résumé writing
Coordinating body movements and monitoring personal fitness		**Focused research and analytic skills**	Selecting, sequencing, analysing and synthesising
Creating and delivering a multimedia persuasive presentation		Goal setting and planning for accomplishment of goals	Speaking well to various audiences in various forums for various purposes
Creating and performing	Interpreting and generating texts in graphical form (e.g. maps, diagrams, charts, timelines, timetables)	Identifying and utilising support structures and agencies	Specialised researching
Creating and presenting a performance accomplished with cultural authenticity	Knowing and applying principles for persuasive display of detailed information, especially in visual forms (diagrammatic, tabular, graphical, …)	Knowing and using conventions and techniques of graphical communication of a building	Understanding 'the economic problem' as it relates to trade
Developing a knowledge of self and one's relationships with surrounding communities		Knowing and using systems for understanding and describing self	Understanding and using historical methodologies (including distinguishing between primary and secondary sources) and appreciating diferences in perspectives/interpretive frameworks
Exploiting the features of web page and other software in making use of an Intranet	Managing events	Knowing and using the discourse of business and trade, in English and another nominated language	
Gathering and evaluating information for a specific purpose	Measuring (with analysis of errors)	Knowing and using the languages of business and employment	Understanding and utilising a design process
Negotiating and working with peers	Negotiating with peers and others	Knowing how mathematics has developed within and among cultures and is used to frame and answer questions of significance, in particular in astronomy	**Understanding various biological and chemical structures and systems, and associated concepts, nomenclatures and notations**
Report writing	Operating/utilising supporting technology		**Understanding what constitute ethical questions and principles**
Selecting, sequencing and structuring information	Producing and performing	**Laboratory practices**	
Taking, collating and making sense of measurements	Promoting a case through an oral or written presentation	Mathematical concepts and techniques	Understanding the Earth's rotation on its axis and revolution around the Sun
Using diagrams to clarify and convey ideas	Understanding and applying design processes	**Organising ideas and data, sifting through them, arranging them wisely and making sense of them**	Using the language of architectural form and style
Viewing, reading and listening	Understanding and appreciating the cultural interests and priorities of a person from another culture	Persuading through speaking in a language other than English (without distortion of factual accuracy)	Utilising a broad range of knowledge — literary, historical, philosophical, scientific, linguistic — to convince and evoke
Working cooperatively to achieve a common goal	Using techniques and skills in construction and model-making		
	Using vocabulary for describing aesthetic effect (e.g. harmony, discord, rhythm, colour)		

Note: The repertoires of practice for Rich Task no. 1 Year 9 (Figure 3.2) are displayed in bold.

and before reporting, there will be competing demands on schools during this period – time for negotiations about standards, remediation of certain students, preparation for transition to the senior school, the tendency to wind down after an assessment point, participation in school-specific curriculum. Different rates of completion will have an impact on teachers and students who transfer between schools and portable student records will be necessary.

A student engaging in the biotechnology RT could explore chemistry, biology, ethics, public health, events management, even philosophy and modern manners. To produce high-quality work students would learn to do some things that are not within the province of a single subject alone: how to keep track of emerging insights, write to famous people, cope with information overload, work through interpersonal conflict, delay expressing an opinion before being fully informed, synthesise information from a variety of disciplines, and so on. The expectation is that all students learn to use their minds well. This is the main reason they go to school – to learn academic and social skills. However, students will need much practice in these skills over many months before they are ready to demonstrate them.

'Planning backwards' does not begin with delineating specific competencies in particular subjects. This is the standard route for outcomes-based planning, inspired by the old pedagogy of breaking knowledge into pieces. Instead the school begins by focusing on a single constructive act unbounded by discipline. The modes employed – writing, enquiry, discussion of texts, problem-solving and experiment – constitute the heart of what it means to be intellectual.

VALIDITY AND RELIABILITY

Wiggins (1991) presents two challenges that are pertinent here:

> To ask about validity is to ask if the task represents the real thing we want to assess. Does it really represent the student's abilities, traits, capacity for long-term work? For example, the SAT is valid because it statistically correlates with later success in college. But does it really represent the things the student can be good at, or just one thing?
>
> Reliability is another question. Would the student get the same score if she took the test again and gave the same performance? Or would different people score it differently? [The scores from] Standardised tests are reliable by design but we question their validity. Exhibitions, on the other hand, are valid but not necessarily reliable. How do we protect students from capricious, biased judgments?

Pitman, Matters and O'Brien (1995) acknowledge the validity–reliability impasse and take the position that validity should not be traded off for reliability but a small dose of the inverse is acceptable. Nevertheless, the New Basics Framework has an appropriate response to the reliability challenge – a system of social moderation (validating teacher judgements by having them ratified by other teachers) that is generally supported by Queensland educators. The system is based on a trio of key aspects enunciated by Pitman, O'Brien and McCollow (1999): standards, evidence and consensus. This trio translates into three general statements:

- use official statements to describe standards at each level;
- use student work as the evidence upon which judgements are made about standards;
- attain consensus among judges that the work matches the pre-stated standards.

The use of these general principles is described later (see page 49).

Panelling

Panelling, a form of content validation, describes a mechanism whereby a variety of people are invited to serve on panels in order to provide collective validity perspectives.

Since the RTs undertaken by students are transdisciplinary, the panelling of their desirable features requires experts with a range of understandings. Ideally, the panel needs to cover:

- discipline or key learning area;
- people with transdisciplinary understanding;
- people with expertise in pedagogy at the particular age-level;
- practitioners in the community;
- educators with expertise in standards-based assessment;
- people who are familiar with the New Basics Project.

Each RT, however, is unique and the critical issues for one might need some types of panellists more than others; further, some individuals are well able to take more than one of these roles. For the biotechnology task, the roles that are highlighted for panel membership are discipline or key learning area experts (biotechnology and ethics) and practitioners in the community (academics who organise conferences). For others, expertise in pedagogy at the particular age level might be highlighted.

The components of each task and their interrelationships are shown in the task specifications. The assessable performances, however, are only those components displayed in undotted boxes (see Figure 3.2, page 41).

The model for assessment of student performance involves identifying the features that are to be scrutinised, and describing the desired standard of performance on each for work to be considered of high quality. The statements that indicate the features and this standard are called the *desirable features*: they demonstrate achievement in the targeted repertoires of practice and/or other aspects signalled within the diagrammatic representation of the task and therefore contribute to the determination of the grade awarded to the student.

The focus of the panel is on the validity of the desirable features for a particular RT. In particular, it considers the following questions about the draft desirable features:

- Do the desirable features ensure that the assessment covers the full range of work in a balanced way? Are the New Basics referents and targeted repertoires properly evident?
- Do the desirable features capture what is valued within the discipline and by associated professionals? Are there aspects of performance that are valued but have not been emphasised sufficiently?
- Are the indicators of high-quality performance in keeping with the demands of the RT and the opportunities it provides for student learning?
- Is the terminology in keeping with that used in the particular taught discipline or associated professions? Does the panel have any reservations or suggestions about the description of the desirable features?
- Can the panel make other suggestions as to how the desirable features might provide information to teachers that will help ensure that teachers and students understand what is valued?

Immersion

The written version of the RT is not the only information available to schools. Further dialogue occurs in face-to-face immersion sessions for teachers. These take place over several days at the beginning of a three-year span.

So how do children from different backgrounds differ in how they think about genetic engineering, personal health issues or the Australian identity? To allow for variety amongst schools and, at the same time, fulfil expectations of state-wide standards, for this purpose too we have a special tuning mechanism: immersion – the gathering of teachers in face-to-face discussions about the intent of the tasks and the implications of the pre-set assessment standards.

METACONSTRUCT

At the time the original RTs were composed (August 1999), they were generally described in words as a selective string of activities. The heading, the meaning of RTs, and the order and nature of the activities, implied purposes and directions for, and relationships among, the activities. There was no intention then that the description of a task would convey the qualities of student work as evidence of engagement in higher-order processes and mastery of advanced skills. The old version of the biotechnology task is shown in Figure 3.3 (below).

Figure 3.3: *Earlier version of Year 9 Rich Task no. 1 – Science and ethics confer*

Biotechnology – emerging issues and trends
Students will show that they are able to debate a range of issues, including ethical and moral questions, to do with emerging scientific advances in biotechnology. They use their knowledge of living organisms to prepare summaries, arguments and counter-arguments to use in public forums. They make reasoned predictions and prepare a plan for a world conference to be held five years hence, taking account of purpose, themes, presenters and audiences.

It was considered that there was value in deconstructing these implied relationships, within and across the RTs, as a means to uncovering the unstated but well-embedded values of the broad range of educationists who had contributed to them.

This deconstruction (Gray, 2000) revealed an underlying learning process – analogous to a design process – together with the enactment of the resulting design generic to virtually all the transdisciplinary tasks. Teachers clearly valued such real-world actions as gathering information through research and consultation and transforming it through analysis and synthesis with the aim of developing a strategy that could be enacted and reflected upon.

The sequence below provides details of this underlying process or metaconstruct. Whereas a single RT may not necessarily involve something from each of these eight groups, the essentials of this metaconstruct invariably surfaced:
• Research: Consult;
• Analyse: Synthesise: Relate: Select;
• Negotiate (with others): Personalise;
• Plan: Design: Create;
• Judge: Decide;

- Operate: Make: Act;
- Evaluate: Revise;
- Present: Perform: Explain: Communicate.

The list format conceals the vital truth that while there is some implied sequence of activities, much of the process relies on how the activities inform and draw meaning from each other. The richness of a task lies as much in this freedom and need to exploit integrated higher-order thinking and performance skills as it does in the range of subject disciplines that are involved and drawn upon.

Further, assessment of performance on an RT is released from assessment of individual performance components *in vacuo*. Instead, the performance component can be viewed in terms of its own distinctive characteristics and the relationships known to be valued among the various types of activity.

TRANSPORTABLE SKILLS

RTs are designed to ensure that students leave school with more than thin scholastic knowledge and that they achieve genuine understanding that can be transferred to new contexts. Good tasks require integrative acts, often calling on students to synthesise their learning in more than one domain and then put it to use, thus highlighting a view of knowledge as integrated perception, cognition and use.

The essential point about targeted repertoires of practice is the extent to which the practices are common to behaviour in different contexts. The assumption is that the mastery of a practice in one context offers the potential of transfer to others. Another assumption is that learning to master a practice within two different contexts is reinforcing. The ultimate test of transportability is not just that skills can be transported but that students can choose the right one (from an acquired repertoire) to import at the right time.

ASSESSMENT, MODERATION AND REPORTING

Transparency in assessment demands pre-existing criteria against which student work will be judged. These criteria will specify desirable features of task performance, but will not be so specific as to discourage discourse, innovation, novelty and local contextualisation.

The desirable features for the biotechnology exemplar task illustrated in Figure 3.2 (page 41) are as follows.

High-quality performance is evidenced by:
- deep understanding and mastery of aspects of *language use* with respect to style, tenor and intention. This task demands language use in the following ways: précis writing, protocols of introduction and formal correspondence; explaining chemical and biological structures and systems with due regard to nomenclature and notations of science;
- accurate and detailed knowledge of a range of *scientific techniques*, and meaningful contribution to laboratory activities;
- *deep analysis* of a biotechnological issue, examined by means of presentation abstracts for six real-life people who can be seen to make distinctive, valuable contributions and who collectively fulfil the conference aim to foster appreciation of the range of views uncovered.

Acceptable performance (successful task completion) is evidenced by:
• identification of the science and ethical implications of an issue in a biotechnological process

Adequate performance (successful task completion) is evidenced by:
• identification of the science and ethical implications of an issue in a biotechnological process.

RT assessment standards are pitched to the second half of Years 3, 6 and 9. They remain the same even if students complete the tasks earlier. One advantage of the variable timing for completion of assessment is that students who finish early can move on to enrichment activities or a more strongly differentiated curriculum. Meanwhile, other students can work on the tasks until the latest date at which assessment can occur, in some cases having repeated aspects of the task that were unsatisfactory. It also encourages teaching and learning in a multi-aged environment. Teachers are able to encourage excellence by expanding the fields of knowledge and repertoires of practice of gifted students beyond those typically acquired by their peers in conventional programmes.

The 'richness' of an RT requires an assessment model that extracts information not only about the quality of the 'product' (the completed task) but also about which desirable intellectual strategies have been used by the student, culminating in the RT. RTs, by definition, are characterised by complexity. By enabling variable and creative responses, they cater for student diversity without compromising standards. Their propositional content is notional but imprecise, maintaining validity while not demanding the rote representation of the same content by all. For these reasons they do not lend themselves to precise quantified or analytic grading, but rather to holistic grading.

Teachers judge student performance on an RT according to holistic assessment against several desirable features, trading off inconsistent performances across features, and assigning an overall grade. Performance is reported holistically (for the completed task), on a scale from A (highest) to C or E (depending on the task) with U (ungraded) applying to the student who does not complete the task or whose work is unsatisfactory.

Although the number of available grades will vary between tasks, this number will not be less than three, for several reasons. Given that RTs are the high-profile educational goals of the system, teachers would be hesitant to fail students. If there is no differentiation in student performance on RTs, why go to so much trouble in the first place? There is consistent educational evidence that higher expectations raise standards of attainment. Students learn more if they are taught more and are expected to perform better as a consequence. A good RT is inherently capable of generating a range of decisions about student performance. This information is worth having.

RTs allow for a range of approaches and outcomes, and are not just linked to expected levels: one feature of this kind of assessment is that students frequently surprise teachers with unexpected levels of understanding.

Comparability of state-wide standards is ensured through public presentations by students and ratification of teacher judgements by other teachers. The general statements about the trio of aspects of a moderation system (standards, evidence and consensus) mentioned earlier in the chapter (page 43) are now restated for the particular case of RTs:

- Develop, with teachers and the community, agreed standards. Compose descriptors of standards. Express these as desirable features for the highest level of those available for each RT.
- For each RT in each school, where appropriate, produce a public exhibition of mastery. Judge the standard of performance against the pre-set descriptors.
- Come to a shared understanding of the meaning of the pre-stated desirable features before students commence work via an immersion session that includes reaching a shared understanding of the meaning of the task itself, accompanied by model plans of attack. Ensure that teachers' judgements are ratified by teachers from other schools.

The aim is to supplement the moderation process with electronic means of communication, which enable easy exchange of text, graphics and video and support continuous conversation.

Reporting of student performance on RTs, to parents and the system, is mandatory at the end of each three-year span. The reults of summative assessment will be reported, in a common format, as an overall grade for each RT – with associated legend for ease of interpretation. State-wide comparability of standards is guaranteed.

CONCLUSION

Queensland's Rich Tasks represent curriculum and assessment intertwined. They involve intellectual habits and life skills that transcend subjects. They deliberately engage with high-stakes discourses – those knowledges, fields and paradigms that have power and salience in researching, analysing and interpreting the world. Some link with traditional ways of doing things; others are new. Some require existing practices and skills, some the blending of old and new. Still others require students and teachers to construct and explore new problems, new learning strategies and new solutions. They represent assessment and pedagogy 'feeding off each other' (Fullan, 1993). They can be a diagnostic tool or a catalyst to stretch the gifted student. They are at the one time an educational device and an assessment strategy. They are sensitive to process as well as product. They depend on the intellect, imagination and expertise of teachers, are motivating to students and are learning activities in themselves. The Framework Research Program will incorporate feedback from teachers on the motivational and transformational powers of RTs. As a new species, the RT has reshaped our approach to assessment in the twenty-first century.

PART II

The Assessment of Mathematical Skills

Overview

Paul Kimmelman

North Central Regional Education Laboratory, USA

The increased emphasis on standards-based curriculum reform, and assessment based on those reforms, has arguably led to improvements in school curricula and student achievement. It is somewhat ironic that they have also created a 'research implementation gap'. This gap is between those who *analyse* educational data and the daily practitioners, teachers and administrators who *use* it. In Part II, Peter Pool, Diane Shorrocks-Taylor, Bronwen Swinnerton and Janice Curry (of the Assessment and Evaluation Unit, University of Leeds, UK) and Linda Jensen Sheffield (of Northern Kentucky University, USA) demonstrate the importance of educational research for informing practice – whilst clearly highlighting the caveat that the research must be used as a tool for planning and not as the sole basis for making instructional decisions. The authors caution us that there may be differences between gifted and advanced learners, that gender may be important when investigating mathematical learning and that a framework for assessment is important if it is intended to improve instruction. Educational research data require considerable analysis and investigation before final conclusions may be drawn.

Nonetheless, the World Class Tests project undertaken by QCA has important implications for mathematics educators. Considerable resources have been devoted to students with special educational needs. However, those needs have been primarily identified as the factors providing obstacles to learning among the least able students, rather than the requirements of the most able students for high-quality mathematical learning experiences. Not nearly as much research has been carried out with the aim of discovering how best to teach the brightest students and understanding what they are capable of learning.

In Chapter 6, Linda Jensen Sheffield offers some provocative thoughts about raising standards, expectations and assessment levels for all students – and more specifically for those who are already in the top 5 per cent achievement band compared to their peers. QCA's World Class Tests project, discussed in Chapters 4 and 5, will help educators improve the quality of mathematics instruction by providing data about what nine and 13 year old students are capable of doing in mathematics and problem solving. More importantly, QCA has taken mathematics assessment beyond the traditional paper-and-pencil and rote memory tasks to incorporate the use of technology and problem solving questions. Whilst they may only touch the 'tip of the iceberg', World Class Tests provide a new approach to assessment that unveils not only answers to questions, but also reveals more about what students understand.

The Part II authors agree that the data from World Class Tests and the Third International Mathematics and Science Study (TIMSS) provide sufficient fuel for the engine of inquiry to better understand differences between students and what they learn. They also agree that the data can be misleading. A good analogy might be a medical test that provides 'false-positive' results, which lead the patient to believe that there is something wrong, when in fact no problem exists. The variables in education research are such that results indicating that a problem exists may be misleading. We can learn more about this type of information in Chapter 5, where Diane Shorrocks-Taylor *et al.* review the issues of gender in relation to mathematics achievement. While these assessments are essential to improving educational practices, it is also important to carefully analyse the data and not draw conclusions from only one study.

The 'research implementation gap', which I described earlier, must be understood by our researchers. High-level intellectual inquiry and debate that does not directly involve classroom teachers and school administrators will not lead to improving instructional practices and curriculum in mathematics classrooms. The researchers should take note of Linda Jensen Sheffield's description of the Kentucky reform plan. She notes (page 86) that, 'Hundreds of teachers from all grade levels and subject areas were called upon to write and revise mission statements, philosophies and goals that everyone could support'. That model should serve as an exemplar for our work on World Class Tests.

As the former President of the First in the World Consortium, discussed in Chapter 6, I can attest to the importance of meaningful educational research used in ways that involve classroom teachers who want to improve their teaching. It may sound like a simple process, but this type of reform effort – whether using research data from a small consortium of school districts or a nation such as England – requires firm leadership, structure, time and the full involvement of the participants.

---

4 A Mathematics Curriculum for the Gifted and Talented

Peter Pool
Assessment and Evaluation Unit (AEU), University of Leeds, UK

THE PURPOSE OF THIS CHAPTER is to shed some light on what able children at age nine and 13 years are able (or unable) to do in mathematics. This will inform the debate on curriculum issues with regard to the gifted and talented in general and, more specifically, the development of World Class Tests. The findings come from development work in the construction of World Class Tests in mathematics by the Assessment and Evaluation Unit (AEU) at the University of Leeds on behalf of QCA.

By way of a health warning, a few words on the nature of test development are in order to set the background for what follows. Test development is not a good way to set a curriculum. A test inevitably influences the taught curriculum in ways that may be both good and bad depending on the quality of the test, the significance of the test results and the professionalism of the teachers. Test development may shed light on the curriculum and reveal which parts of the curriculum are being taught badly or not at all. However, test development is narrow and reduces rich classroom experience to what can be captured by pencil and paper (or mouse and computer screen). We are all losers if what is taught is confined to what can be presented in a test.

To reinforce the point, it has been noticeable in our search for assessment material for World Class Tests how unproductive the trawl of websites, published paper sources and so forth has been in offering content suitable as assessment material. There is, apparently, the very reasonable view prevailing that catering for the gifted and talented is about rich activities rather than assessment and this is not something I would question. I would argue, however, that assessment has a role in sharpening up teaching and bringing into focus some aspects of students' understanding.

A Test Developer's Lot

Test developers have to work within three major constraints (as well as a million minor ones), which are at times mutually antagonistic and at other times mutually supportive:

For brief notes on the UK education system, please see page 127.

- students' cognitive abilities;
- educational values of society at large;
- mathematical orthodoxy.

None of these can be trusted. We have only vague and incomplete maps of children's cognition. The usual metaphors of filling empty vessels, growing plants etc. are perniciously inadequate in characterising how children know something one day but not the next. Educational values are notoriously fickle: this year's good practice will soon become the bad old ways of a bygone age as we chase the chimera of getting things right. Furthermore, mathematical orthodoxy is split into factions when it comes to critical definitions of professional language. A successful test may be the one which offends the least; a good test is one which distracts the critics – and is altogether more rare.

Although the test may be a bad master, it can nevertheless be a good servant. Test development is, at the end of the day, a dialogue with children – in which we try to recognise the range and depth of their thinking. A good mathematics question is like a good joke: it taps into someone's imagination. In doing so, it sheds light and reveals a little of their understanding of the subject and their wider perceptions of the world.

Who are the gifted and talented in mathematics?

HMI (1992) admit that *'There is no generally accepted definition of what constitutes a very able or gifted child'* (p.1; quoted in Kennard, 1996).

Our own surveys of teachers suggest that the gifted and talented in mathematics:
- enjoy numbers, can understand and manipulate them, and enjoy the challenges they provide;
- are intrigued by mathematics, and recognise the structure and relationships of the subject;
- have considerable mental agility – they can hold a chain of operations in their head;
- have confidence and are methodical, they persevere;
- can communicate both orally and in written form... can give explanations in mathematical language;
- can apply and adapt knowledge to new situations – can transfer skills across knowledge areas;
- have the skills to tackle open-ended problems and are good problem solvers.

(AEU, 1999)

Conventional curricula for school mathematics are broad rather than deep. This is not entirely surprising in a curriculum intended to support the general education of the many, where a motivating subject interest cannot be taken for granted. It is likely to be easier to introduce the somewhat sham pearls of bright new topics at a shallow level making modest intellectual demand on students, rather than push for a deeper understanding of familiar old ones. This approach is not well suited to the most able, who will quickly grasp concepts and remain unsatisfied by the fact that they are not applied in an intellectually stimulating context.

In developing a mathematics curriculum for World Class Tests, we have interpreted the above as implying that an appropriate curriculum for the gifted and talented would be based upon generalised intellectual skills of insight, deduction and so forth, rather than knowledge of mathematical topics *per se*. A curriculum in mathematics cannot be 'topic free'. We have chosen to avoid as far as possible the curriculum edge. Instead, we stay within safely-known topics whilst demanding insight and confidence rather than regurgitation of known procedures. In other words we are seeking to identify the *able* mathematician rather than the *advanced* one.

There are a number of reasons for this view:

- A curriculum of extended topics would almost certainly encourage test candidates and their teachers to pursue shallow coverage and 'force-feeding' of memorised procedures without a great deal of understanding.
- At a practical level, particularly in international contexts, there is considerable variation in the timing and range of mathematics teaching. Whilst there are broad similarities between countries in the flavour of mathematics covered by, say, grades 1 to 3, or 4 to 6, there are specific variations within these currents: when, for example, are negative numbers or percentages introduced and how far are they taught? (TIMSS, 1997).
- Children need a well-founded curriculum base to demonstrate their insight, mental agility and so forth and this would not be facilitated by having to struggle with new, undigested ideas and concepts.

To expand on this last point, we have sought to avoid items whose difficulty lies not so much in the insight demanded, but in the unfamiliarity with what later becomes routine. Our initial exploratory trialling has been in English schools following the national curriculum. Pythagoras's theorem is a piece of mathematics that some students have recently learnt at this stage, whilst others have not. It is a piece of mathematics that the uninitiated would find virtually impossible to deduce (unless they were mathematicians of Pythagorean calibre); most students find even a straightforward application of it quite difficult during the early stages of exposure. Yet a short while later it becomes mundane mathematics for able children. It is not therefore a reliable means of assessing mathematical insight in 13 year olds. Similar issues arise with, say, the algorithmic addition of fractions at age nine.

In England the National Numeracy Strategy (NNS) has clarified which parts of the curriculum should be taught to the majority of nine year olds. The situation is less clear with 13 year olds, since teaching programmes between the end of key stage 2 and the end of key stage 3 vary enormously from school to school. The extension of the NNS into the secondary years will bring a change in this in the next few years, but to date it has been an empirical exercise to find out which mathematical topics are appropriate for assessment at age 13.

Age nine

The curriculum base for nine year olds is quite small though, as explained above, relatively well defined in England. Nine year old children are making significant cognitive gains during the school year, even in their ability to deal with what is rapidly becoming familiar mathematics. There is, however, cognitive instability, even in bright children: what is apparently grasped today is not clear tomorrow but may reappear confidently next week. This, along with their sensitivity to language, means that the writing and trialling of items for nine year olds requires careful attention to detail.

Language is a particularly difficult issue. There is no obvious justification for expecting a world class mathematician to be a world class linguist, but at the other extreme we have to consider how world class a mathematician can be if he or she cannot communicate effectively. Mathematics as a cultural expression is surely rooted in language. Written mathematics can be seen as a precise and elegantly economic expression of ideas, but without the means to talk about it, it cannot develop. I think we must be wary of the child who has mastered abstract algorithms and so appears able to 'do mathematics' but cannot understand the question that requires the algorithm.

In World Class Test development we aim to minimise language demand and remove unnecessary obstacles to the mathematics, whilst recognising that a significant part of mathematics is that of making the link between common language use and a mathematical formulation of a problem. We also note that the characteristics of mathematically able children as referred to above include the ability to communicate mathematics: they can talk shop. Provided we do not overvalue this skill, it would seem appropriate to include it in an exploratory development of assessment.

COMMUNICATION SKILLS IN MATHEMATICS

One of our investigations has been into how able nine year olds might cope with so-called 'Explain…' questions. We formulated four such questions, as listed below. Examples of children's responses will be discussed in the pages that follow.

Explain in words how to find out if a number is a multiple of 3. (See page 57.)

Explain in words how to find the number which is exactly half way between two other numbers, A and B. (See page 58.)

Explain in words how to draw an isosceles triangle using just a pencil and a ruler. (See page 59.)

Explain in words why two odd numbers always add up to an even number. (See page 60.)

Children's language has an alluring charm, but from an assessment point of view, the charms must be resisted and the items must satisfy two criteria:

• Can correct responses be distinguished from incorrect ones?
• Is there an acceptable proportion of children offering a correct response?

The decision as to what is a correct response is not trivial. If we are asking children to use language we must match our expectations to what the majority of the trialling sample are capable of writing. When this feels like too much of a compromise of the mathematics, we may well have to lose the question. The mark scheme for a question that only offers the ideal response is not helpful; it must offer the range of acceptable responses that are likely to occur, from the minimally acceptable onwards.

Equally, the difficulty of the item must be considered. Too many or too few children succeeding will mean that the assessment tells us very little, as is illustrated by the examples that follow.

Question: Explain in words how to find out if a number is a multiple of 3

In the acceptable responses, there were notions of dividing the number by 3 (and implicitly or explicitly, checking on the remainder), or adding the digits together and checking whether the total is 3, 6 or 9.

> (bu) It must have 3 gone into it evenly how ever many times and no remainders:

> well if you think its a multiple of 3 you should be able to share it by 3 and no remainder:

> you add the ten digit and the unit digit and if the answer to the 9,6 or 3 it is but if the sum ends up in a tow digit number add those tow number together.

Less satisfactory is:

You can find a multiple of three by doing your three times table.

This is a matter of judgement, of course. It can be argued that if you have a long enough view of 'the three times table' then all the multiples of 3 will be in it (by definition, to an adult mind, though perhaps not to a nine year old one). Then there is the practicality of this approach: is the child writing the above envisaging only the numbers up to, say, 36? Have they grasped the generality of the question? No-one knows. We make a tentative judgement for the moment.

More obviously confused is:

If you want to find out if a number is a multiple of 3 you find out if it is an odd number or times it by 3.

The overall facility for this was about 35 per cent of the target group, which makes a viable question, given the clarity of responses.

Question: Explain in words how to find the number which is exactly half way between two other numbers, A and B

This produced some very clear responses:

> Take the two numbers A and B
> add them together and divide
> them by two

> Do Do Double Both ~~~ numben
> ~~~ then half ~~~ them then add
> the two half half ooth numbe
> and then add the halfed numbers
> together

Quite intriguing are a number of visual approaches:

> Find how much space there is between
> A and B, halve it and find where it is.

> You have to take the biggest number from
> the other number, to get the
> answer then divide the answer in half

Perhaps too specific (and annoyingly in error) is:

> If you want to find half
> way between 20 – 30 you
> have to count up to where you
> can count up to 30 and down
> to 20 equaly the answer is 35

Whether this is too specific is open to debate. One can almost read the words 'for example' written between the lines and feel the child struggling to speak in general terms. Equally one might argue this to be an entirely unjustified inference, which in any case sets criteria that could never be sustained in a larger setting, with large numbers of markers trying to grasp such diffuse sentiments.

Only 5 per cent of the sample gave suitable responses even in crude terms, which rules it out as a test item in its present form.

Question: Explain in words how to draw an isosceles triangle using just a pencil and a ruler

This separated children out into those few who understood isosceles triangles in terms of generalised mathematical properties and those who had a visual impression of them, all very much undermined by the lack of clarity of expression.

Examples of the former are:

two
One side of your tringal should be the same lengh but one side should be a diffrent Sc get a ruler do two lines about 45.cm and the outher one acout 90cm.

you get a rula and Draw two lines the same lenght joint together and the draw anougher line out the end of ther two lines

And some of the many examples of the latter are:

draw an upside down v shape and join the two bottoms to – get her.

Make the top bit pointy and draw it fatter as you go down.

You use your ruler to draw a bent line another one then do a straight one

Note that 'bent' probably means sloping and 'straight' probably means vertical in childspeak – though one would be less likely to infer that without the diagram.

you get your ruler and do an almost strait line pointing right an almost sarait line pointig Left and as Straıgh Line conecting them

These examples reveal the inherent ambiguity of the question, which asks for a description of how to draw an isosceles triangle. It does not, literally, ask for the general case, even though adults may feel they 'know' that this is required. Nine year olds, not versed in the sophisticated use of language that adults take for granted, can with some justification claim that anything which *looks like* an isosceles triangle will be one – there is no need to resort to first principles.

It is unlikely that the wording can be significantly improved. Asking for the generalised mathematical properties of an isosceles triangle, in those words, would not make much sense to this age group and is in any case just as ambiguous as the previous formulation. Asking what makes an isosceles triangle different from other triangles is gloriously open and invites the imagination to run riot. And so we face the conclusion that knowing mathematics inevitably involves some linguistic skills and awareness of how language is used.

Only 8 per cent of the sample could give a suitably accurate and unambiguous response, which makes it a hard question to include in a test.

Question: Explain in words why two odd numbers always add up to an even number

This one is hard even for adults, and it produced a wide range of approaches from nine year olds:

There is the enigmatic:

It Because they cancel each other out.

Or the more explicit:

...Two odd number equal an even number because if you add 6+6 it equals 12 but you have 7+7 it makes 14 because you have an extra 1 on each number

Or the logical argument (not quite correct, but good going for nine year olds):

Because you have to have 3 odd numbers to have a odd answer

Facilities on this question were only 5 per cent, again ruling it out for test purposes in its current format.

ALGEBRAIC THINKING

One would not expect to see any formal expression of algebraic thinking by nine year olds. This does not mean that they have no capacity to think algebraically – merely that they have not mastered (or been taught) the formal modes of mathematical expression. But it is of course interesting to see what intuitive, informal expression can be found, if we can pitch a question at a suitable level. We used the question shown in Figure 4.1 as an attempt to discern this.

Figure 4.1: *Algebra question, version 1*

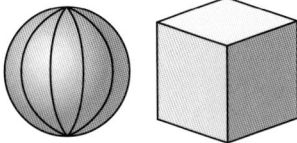

A ball and a cube together weigh 150 grams.
3 balls and 5 cubes weigh 530 grams.
What is the weight of a ball?

This produced a disappointing 2.5 per cent facility amongst the target group with 75 grams (presumably $150 \div 2$) as by far the most popular answer, suggesting a failure to engage with the problem in any depth.

We rewrote the question to offer some visual cues, as shown in Figure 4.2.

Figure 4.2: *Algebra question, version 2*

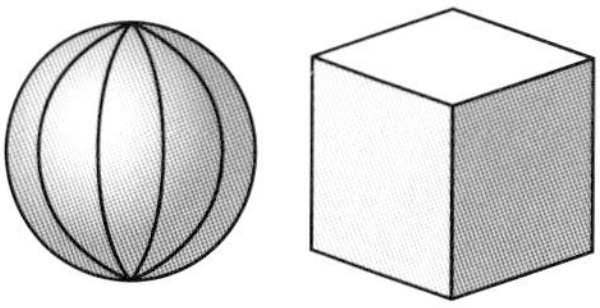

A ball and a cube weigh 170 grams.
Three balls and two cubes weigh 420 grams.

What is the weight of one cube?
Show your working.

This produced an improved facility though still only 6 per cent with a correct answer and a further 6 per cent with an incorrect answer but evidence of an appropriate method implying that 12 per cent showed they could meaningfully tackle the question.

The favourite answer was now 85 grams (equivalent to the 75 grams of the earlier version). Few picked up the visual clues in the diagrams and performed a substitution. But now, having asked children to show their working, we had some evidence of how they had gone about answering the question: mostly by trial and occasionally showing some improvement:

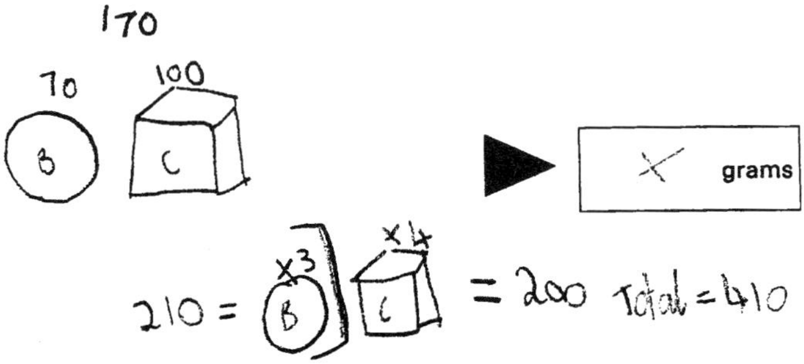

As such the question is almost usable at the difficult end of a test.

Age 13

At age 13, there is more cognitive stability and a broader, less well defined, curriculum. In the English mathematics curriculum, indices are generally known, but not the rules for calculating with them. Formal algebra is an established part of the curriculum at 13 but usually it is not so familiar that children see it as a first resort in formulating their strategies. Our experience to date has been that they do not at this age 'think in formal algebra' in the way that more advanced mathematicians often take as a given. 'Similarity of shapes' is also not commonly known at age 13.

There is a popular view that sees algebraic expression as the hallmark of an able mathematician. We have not found this to be the case, at least at age 13. Thirteen year olds still have quite a bit in common with their nine year old siblings and even able ones often prefer trial and improvement, as can be seen in the example that follows.

Question: Finding the numbers in a sequence

A sequence of seven numbers has a total of 49.
Each number is 6 less than the one before it.
What is the first number in the sequence?
Show your working.

By far the commonest approach to this is trial and improvement, with some 20 per cent getting the correct answer (by any method) and a further 5 per cent showing evidence of a feasible method, but without a correct answer:

Here is a rare approach using formal algebra:

$$n + (n+6) + (n+12) + \cdots$$
$$n + (n-6) + (n-12) + (n-18)$$
$$1, 2, 3, 4, 5, 6$$
$$\frac{\cdot 42}{2} = 21$$
$$\times \frac{\div 1}{6}$$
$$126$$
$$\times \cdot 7n - 126 = 49$$
$$7n = 126 + 49$$
$$7n = 175$$
$$n = 175 \div 7$$
$$= 25$$

▶ $\boxed{\overline{26}\ 25}$

One can question whether the algebraic approach is evidence of mathematical insight and talent or a standard application of an advanced mathematical technique: algebra as the near universal can-opener of mathematics. This may be the sign of the advanced mathematician, rather than the very able one. For an insightful solution we might consider this:

$$\frac{49}{7} = 7 \downarrow$$

$$25 \quad 19 \quad 13 \quad \textcircled{7} \quad 1 \quad -5 \quad -11$$

▶ $\boxed{25}$

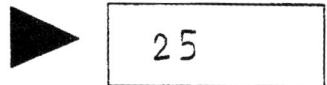

This student appears to be suggesting that the mean of the seven numbers will be the middle one of the sequence, since they form a regular arithmetic sequence. Once the mean is calculated, it is no more than a matter of adding or subtracting 6 in either direction to create the sequence. Overall, this student's test performance was better than that of the algebraicist.

HOW MUCH INSIGHT CAN YOU EXPECT?

The question based on the diagram of two overlapping circles (see Figure 4.3) requires no advanced knowledge of mathematical techniques and very little working needs to be done. Instead, it appears to rely on deep visual insight... so deep that only 5 per cent of the sample could answer it correctly.

We have reworked this question in many ways: using percentages rather than fractions, different shapes, giving the fraction of each circle and asking for the fraction of the whole diagram, but always the facility is about 5 per cent or worse.

Figure 4.3: *Overlapping circles question*

Here are twin identical overlapping circles.

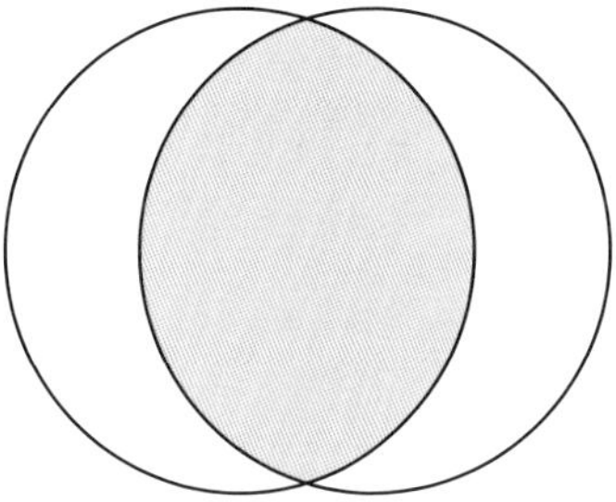

$\frac{3}{5}$ of the whole diagram is shaded.

What fraction of each circle is shaded?

Conclusions

I offer here a number of observations as a contribution to the debate over a curriculum for the gifted and talented:
- We must be careful to distinguish the gifted mathematician from the advanced one. We should be looking for depth rather than spread of knowledge, though it may be harder to achieve this.
- Communication skills, the ability to talk about one's thinking in mathematics, is a rich and revealing area, even with nine year old children. Language will always be a sensitive issue, but we should not let anxieties about language competence obscure this important area of communication in mathematics.
- In looking at the mathematical performance of older students, we should not be dazzled by sophisticated presentations such as fluent expression of algebra, welcome though this may be. We must keep our eyes on insight as much as on technical proficiency.

5 Mathematics assessment in the World Class Tests: some gender issues

Diane Shorrocks-Taylor, Bronwen Swinnerton and Janice Curry

Assessment and Evaluation Unit (AEU), University of Leeds, UK

PARTICIPATION IN THE UK WORLD CLASS TESTS PROJECT HAS ENCOURAGED US to consider in greater depth a range of issues in relation to the performance and attainment of talented mathematicians at ages nine and 13. The World Class Tests are designed to assess higher-level mathematical thinking, not necessarily directly related to the national curriculum in England, nor to curricula in other countries. Instead, they seek to address the skills of wider understanding of mathematical ideas, the application of existing concepts to novel situations, the unusual combining of mathematical ideas and mathematical insight (see Chapter 4, page 53). The tests are at present being developed in both paper-based and computer-based versions, but it is findings in relation to paper-based testing that will be the major focus here.

Background

In England, the introduction of a national curriculum in core and foundation subjects (nine in all) with mandatory national testing of all students in the core subjects (English, mathematics and science) at ages seven, 11 and 14, means that we are in a position to evaluate performance year on year in a range of ways. These national testing data have been available now since 1996, revealing two major trends, namely: an overall rise in performance at most key stages since 1996, and a general improvement in the performance of girls in particular over this period. This latter trend is now signalled in newspaper headlines and indeed the problem of boys' poor attainment has considerable educational and political significance. This of course must be set alongside the wider finding that the scores of boys, especially in mathematics, tend to be at the two extremes of the distribution. In England, the

For brief notes on the UK education system, please see page 127.

Department for Education and Skills has a website dedicated to gender and achievement, with special emphasis on 'boys' underachievement' (see DfES, 2000). This is, of course, a very different situation from three decades ago, when the poor attainment of girls was the focus.

NATIONAL TESTING DATA AND THE PERFORMANCE OF BOYS AND GIRLS

To illustrate these general and highly publicised trends, Figures 5.1 to 5.9 (pages 68 to 72) show the data for national test scores in English, mathematics and science at key stage 1 (seven year olds – no science testing at this age), key stage 2 (11 year olds), key stage 3 (14 year olds). It should be emphasised that these tests are curriculum-based, assessing the required curriculum in the core subjects. By way of further explanation, at each of the key stages, there is a 'benchmark' level (an expected level of attainment), namely level 2 at key stage 1, level 4 at key stage 2 and level 5 at key stage 3.

Figures 5.1 to 5.9 show the trend of generally rising standards of attainment since 1996 (though less so for key stage 3) and it is these three age groups that are closest to those of the World Class Tests. The Figures also show the sustained higher performance of girls, especially in English. In mathematics and science, the differences are much smaller and less consistent. The situation for the GCSE scores (16 year olds) reflects a similar pattern, in that for all subjects taken together, girls are outperforming boys (particularly in English); the situation in mathematics again (as for key stages 2 and 3) shows girls holding their own against the boys.

Figure 5.1: *Key stage 1 (seven year olds) 'benchmark' results for boys and girls in reading comprehension, 1996 to 2000 (required benchmark, level 2 or above)*

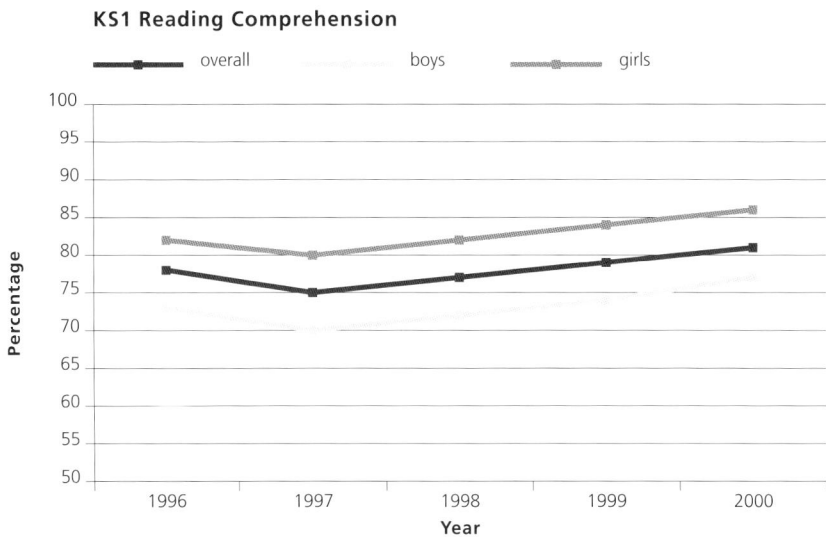

Figure 5.2: *Key stage 1 (seven year olds) 'benchmark' results for boys and girls in mathematics, 1996 to 2000 (required benchmark, level 2 or above)*

KS1 Mathematics

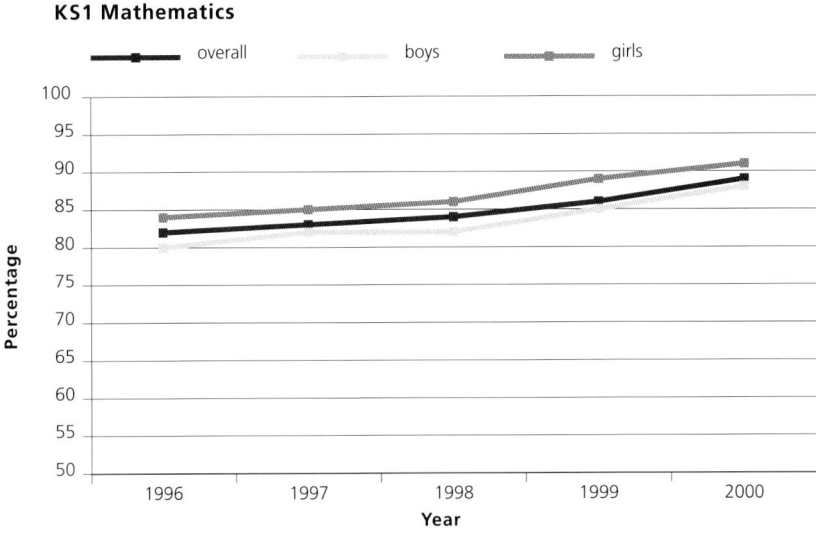

Figure 5.3: *Key stage 2 (11 year olds) 'benchmark' results for boys and girls in English, 1996 to 2000 (required benchmark, level 4 or above)*

KS2 English

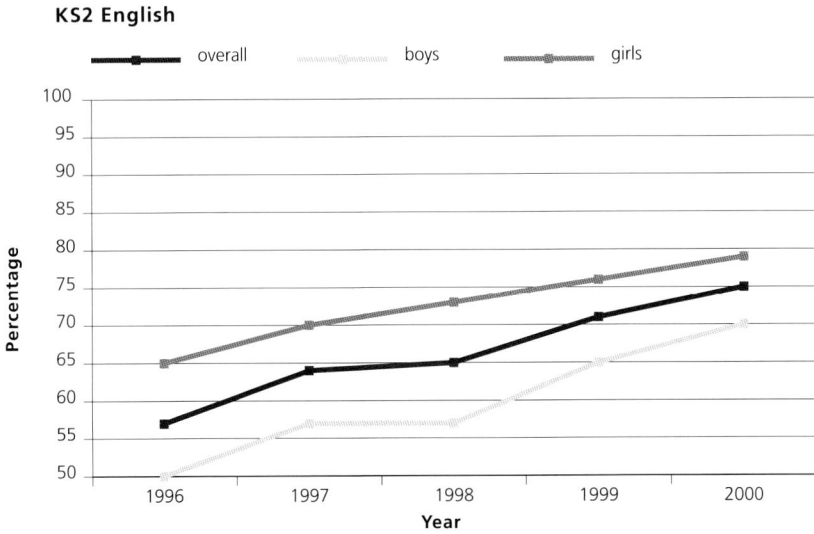

Figure 5.4: *Key stage 2 (11 year olds) 'benchmark' results for boys and girls in mathematics, 1996 to 2000 (required benchmark, level 4 or above)*

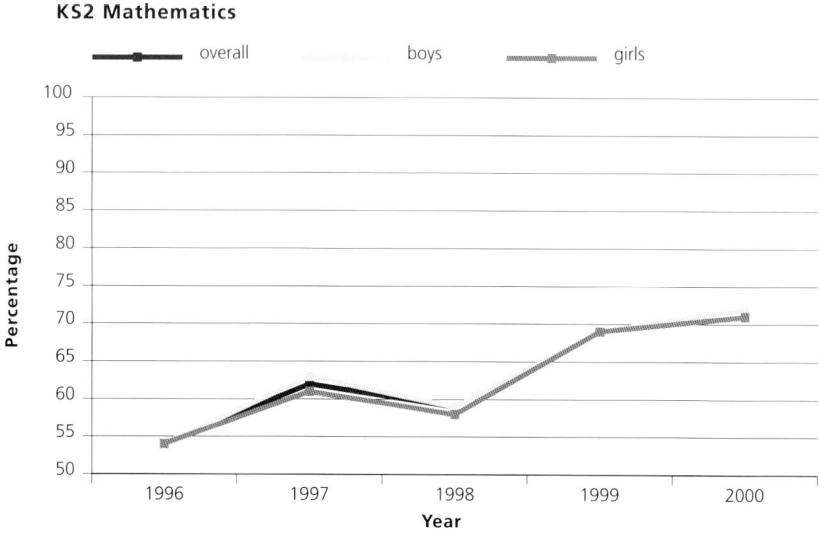

KS2 Mathematics

Figure 5.5: *Key stage 2 (11 year olds) 'benchmark' results for boys and girls in science, 1996 to 2000 (required benchmark, level 4 or above)*

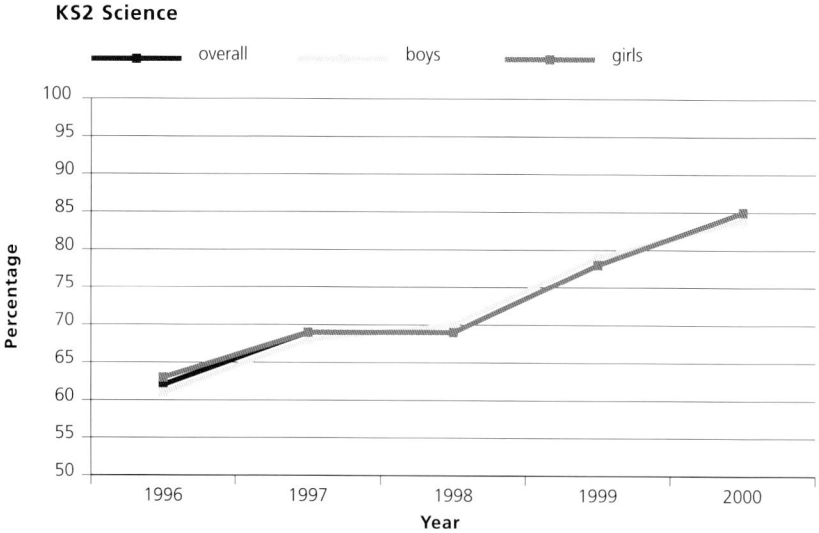

KS2 Science

Figure 5.6: *Key stage 3 (14 year olds) 'benchmark' results for boys and girls in English, 1996 to 2000 (required benchmark, level 5 or above)*

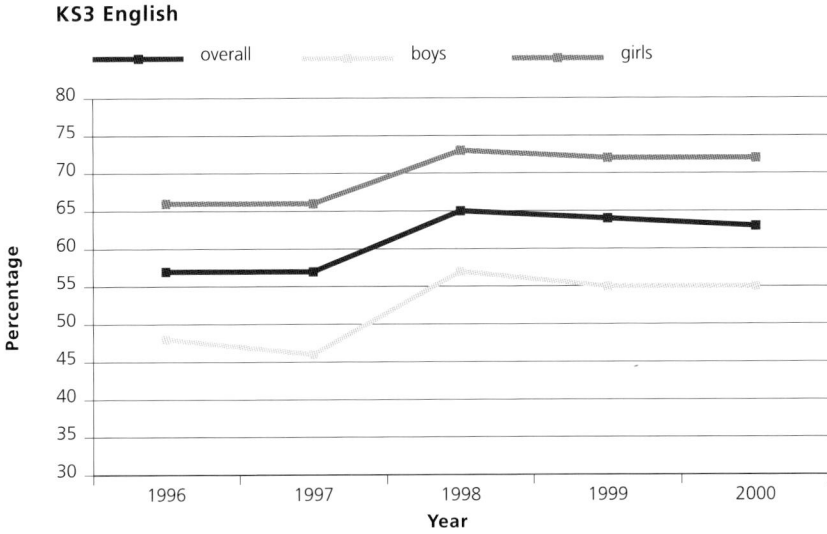

Figure 5.7: *Key stage 3 (14 year olds) 'benchmark' results for boys and girls in mathematics, 1996 to 2000 (required benchmark, level 5 or above)*

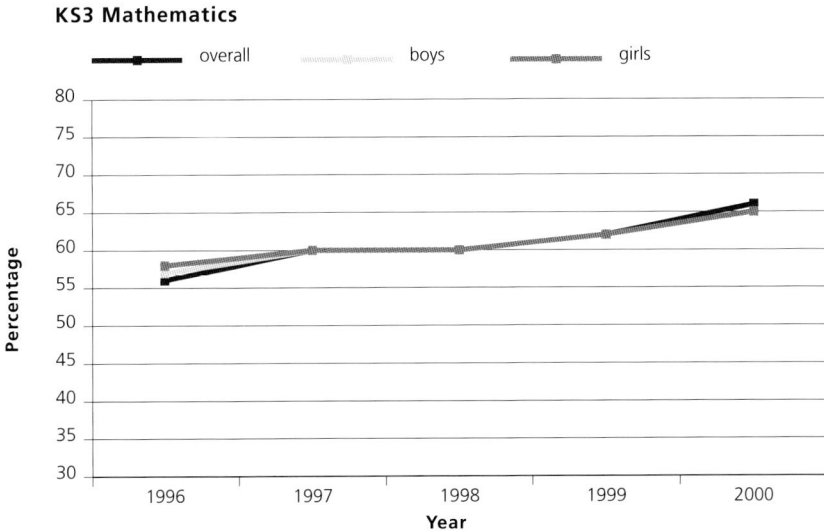

Figure 5.8: *Key stage 3 (14 year olds) 'benchmark' results for boys and girls in science, 1996 to 2000 (required benchmark, level 5 or above)*

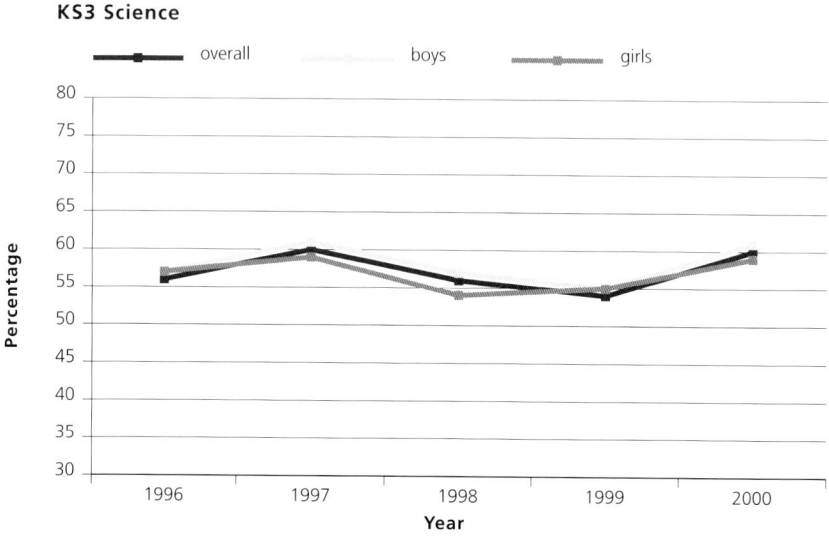

KS3 Science

Figure 5.9: *General Certificate of Secondary Education (GCSE) Grade C to A* results for boys and girls in English, mathematics and overall (2000 only)*

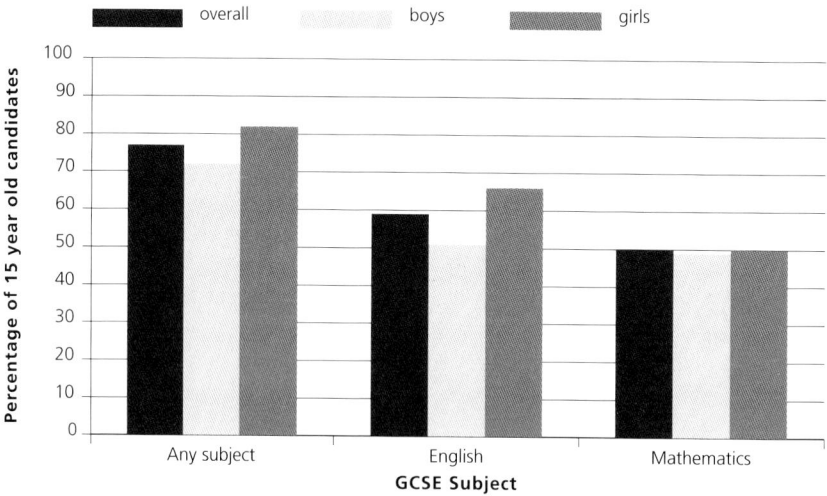

World Class Tests

THE FINDINGS FROM THE WORLD CLASS TESTS IN MATHEMATICS

However, our preliminary findings for performance in mathematics in the World Class Tests at both nine and 13 indicate a rather different pattern, with boys outperforming girls at the upper end of this already selected high attainment range. The results presented here are based on a large scale national pre-test which took place in late October 2000. A total of 948 (470 boys and 478 girls) nine year olds and 1,118 (567 boys and 551 girls) 13 year olds took part, with a total of nine test booklets across the two age groups and 108 test questions. Overall performance data for the two groups is given in Table 5.1 below.

Table 5.1: *Mean scores and standard deviations of boys and girls in the World Class Tests October pre-test (paper-based), all booklets combined*

GENDER	SAMPLE SIZE	MEAN SCORE	STANDARD DEVIATION
Nine year olds			
Boys	467	7.23	3.87
Girls	480	6.81	3.64
13 year olds			
Boys	567	9.08	4.65
Girls	551	7.16	3.84

When all the data were combined, two analyses were done: a straightforward histogram of the results and an analysis by percentile which revealed the following findings, shown in Figures 5.10 and 5.11 (nine year olds) and 5.12 and 5.13 (13 year olds).

Figures 5.10 to 5.13 (pages 73 to 75) tell parallel stories for both these age groups: the boys are outperforming the girls in these mathematics tests at the higher attainment levels. The differences reach statistical significance for the 13 year olds (p=.000) and at the 90 per cent level for the nine year olds (p= .090).

Figure 5.10: *Histogram showing the distribution of scores in the mathematics tests for nine year old boys and girls, all data combined*

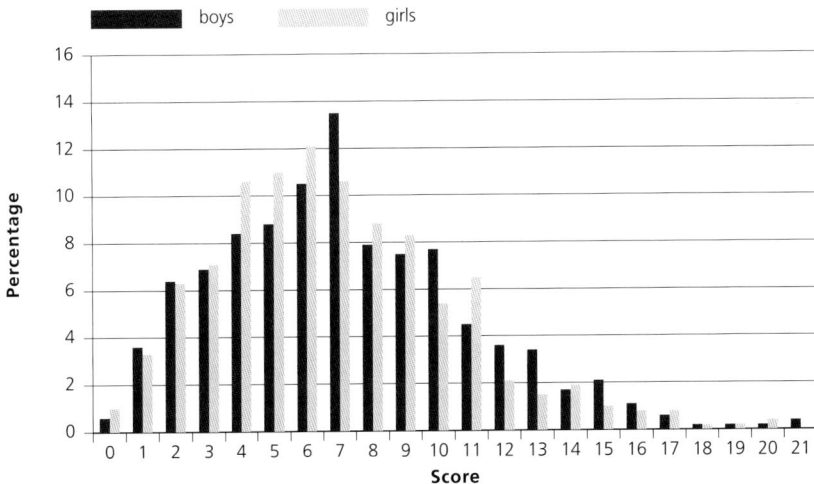

Figure 5.11: *Graph showing percentile scores for nine year old girls and boys in the mathematics tests, all data combined*

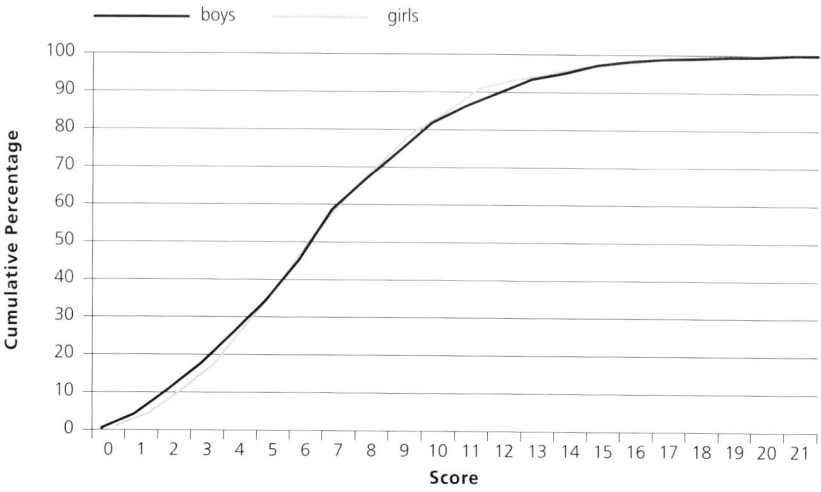

Figure 5.12: *Histogram showing the distribution of scores in the mathematics tests for 13 year old boys and girls, all data combined*

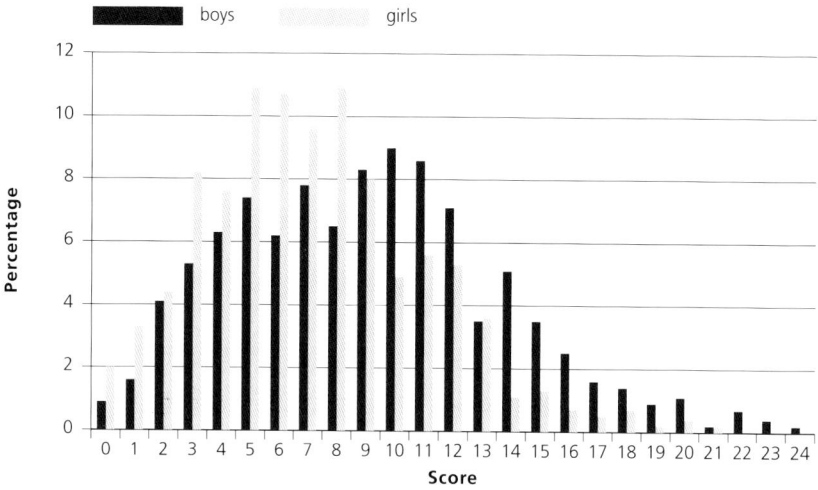

Figure 5.13: *Graph showing percentile scores for girls and boys in the mathematics tests for 13 year olds, all data combined*

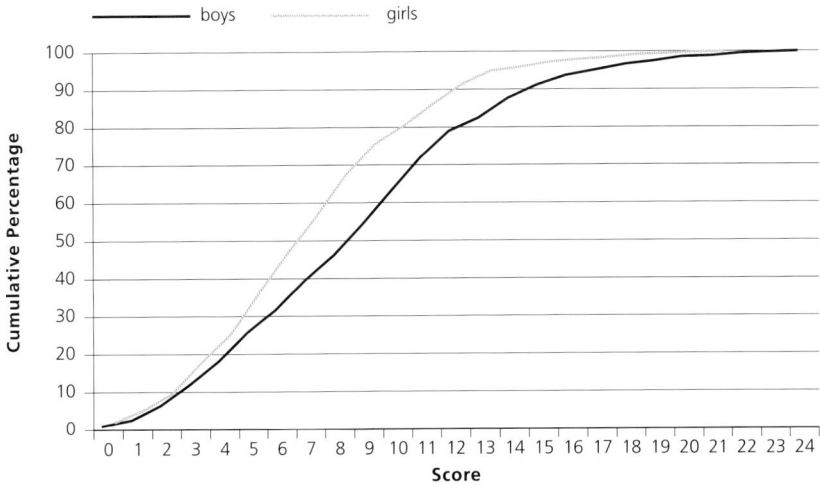

So why should the World Class Tests data be telling a rather different story from the national tests data? Our response was to return to the national tests data and to ask more detailed questions of it. The information presented earlier, in Figures 5.1 to 5.9, shows the general benchmark achievements, which do not focus on performance at the higher levels in each of these relevant age groups. This additional information is shown in Figures 5.14 to 5.16 below. These graphs show attainment at the highest levels in mathematics for each of the key stages.

Figure 5.14: *The attainments of boys and girls at the highest levels in mathematics (level 3+ at key stage 1) for 1996 to 2000*

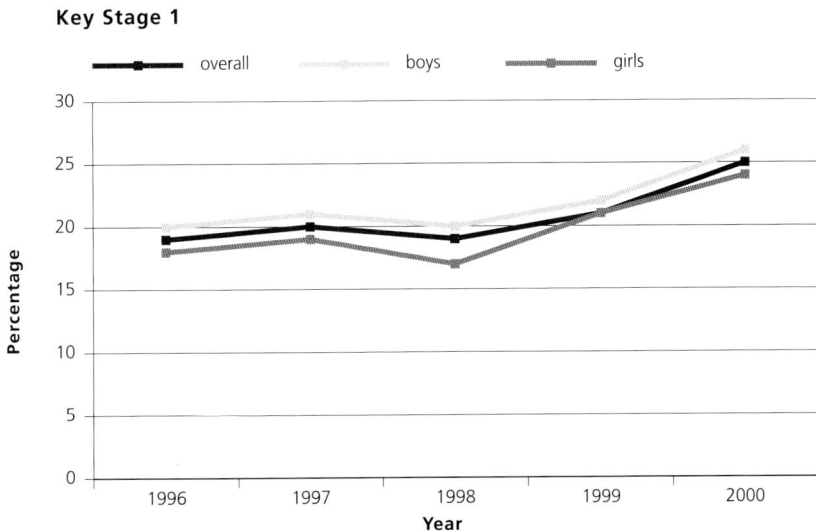

Figure 5.15: *The attainments of boys and girls at the highest levels in mathematics (level 5+ at key stage 2) for 1996 to 2000*

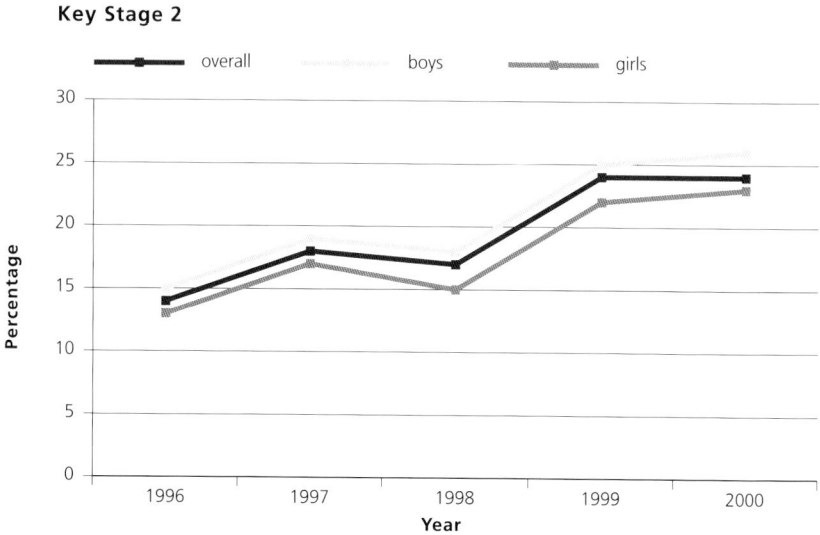

Key Stage 2

Figure 5.16: *The attainments of boys and girls at the highest levels in mathematics (levels 7/8+ at key stage 3) for 1996 to 2000*

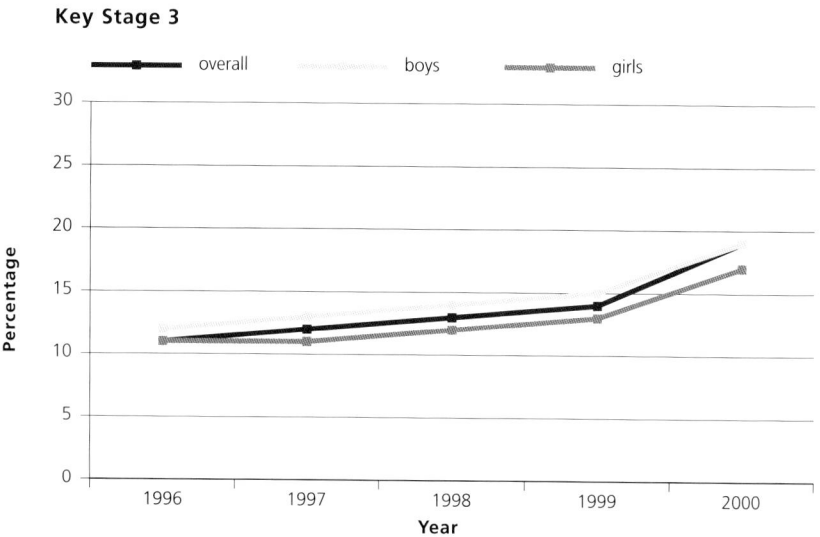

Key Stage 3

This more detailed analysis now begins to make sense of the findings in the World Class Tests samples. In the national data for mathematics, at the highest attainment levels it is the boys who outperform the girls.

One final piece of information is the results of the TIMSS-R exercise (Ruddock, 2000) for 13 year olds, which show that in the English sample, the boys overall outperformed the girls, with the girls' scores declining between 1995 and 1999. This is shown in Figure 5.17 (page 77).

Figure 5.17: *The TIMSS-R results for boys and girls in mathematics, 1995 and 1999 compared*

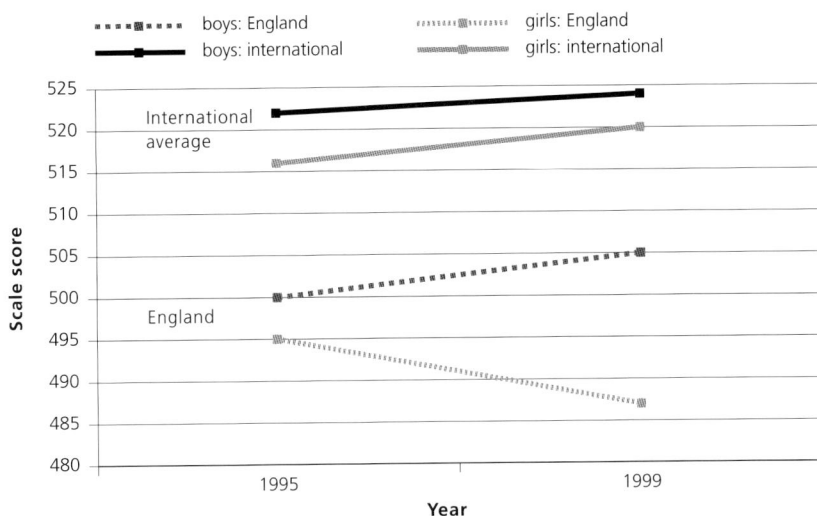

DISCUSSION

The data presented and discussed here reveals that girls are indeed achieving strongly in the core subjects of the national curriculum in England, and in other subjects too, such that the underachievement of boys has become a significant educational and political problem. Even in the traditional 'male' disciplines of mathematics and science, girls are generally holding parity with boys, according to our national test data (mandatory testing) and at GCSE. However, in mathematics this general trend masks an interesting finding, highlighted by the emerging data from the World Class Tests. Boys significantly outnumber girls at the highest levels of attainment, a little publicised fact. Why should this be? Several hypotheses can be suggested and explored in order to account for this finding.

1. The format and content of the questions

The questions in these tests are in a variety of formats and no traditional multiple choice-type questions are included. In the course of completing any test, students are likely to be asked to calculate, complete number sequences, fill in number grids, decide lines of symmetry, work out co-ordinates and many other responses. This is very much in the tradition of the national curriculum tests in the UK. This means that traditional (if now somewhat dated) findings on multiple choice questions, that boys outperform girls (Newbould and Scanlon, 1981; Murphy, 1982) cannot be applied. However, we have no firm research evidence on format effects in relation to gender for other response types. Perhaps this should be the next step in research.

2. The content of the questions

If format effects do not apply, perhaps the content areas covered in the questions are favouring boys. An analysis of the questions where significant gender effects were found reveals that there may be some evidence of clustering in particular curriculum areas. This information is shown in Table 5.2, page 78. Questions were categorised according to which aspects of mathematics seemed to be needed in achieving a solution. Questions categorised as 'geometry' included those that required some form of visual analysis:

77

however, the solution to many of these also required an element of algebra or measures.

Table 5.2: *The content areas of questions where the performance of boys or girls was significantly higher, for nine year olds and 13 year olds*

NINE YEAR OLD ITEMS (9* ASSESSMENT POINTS OUT OF 112) ALL IN FAVOUR OF BOYS					
Number	Fractions	Geometry	Measures	Algebra	Handling Data
4	5	–	–	1	2
13 YEAR OLD ITEMS IN FAVOUR OF BOYS (37* ASSESSMENT POINTS OUT OF 127)					
Number	Fractions	Geometry	Measures	Algebra	Handling Data
1	9	23	9	6	4
13 YEAR OLD ITEMS IN FAVOUR OF GIRLS (2* ASSESSMENT POINTS OUT OF 127)					
Number	Fractions	Geometry	Measures	Algebra	Handling Data
1	–	–	–	–	1

Some assessment points involve more than one content area and are therefore counted twice.

Summarising the findings, the following points can be made.

• At age nine, there were few significant differences (approximately 8 per cent of the assessment points), but all in favour of boys, with the greater proportion in the content areas of 'number' and 'fractions';

• At age 13, most significant differences were in favour of boys, (approximately 30 per cent of the assessment points);

• At age 13, 44 per cent of the questions that produced significant differential performance in favour of boys were in the content area of geometry, involving some form of visual analysis of a geometric situation, and a further 17 per cent were in the related content area of measures.

Further evidence in this connection comes from the TIMSS-R results (Ruddock, 2000), where a similar pattern of results was found. Figure 5.18 (page 79) compares the performance on the English sample (13 to 14 year olds) with the International Average scores in each of the mathematics content areas.

Figure 5.18 shows that, for this age group (13 to 14 year olds):

• boys outperformed girls in every content area both internationally and in England, but the gender differences were greater in England;

• students in the England sample performed consistently higher than the international average in all content areas except geometry;

• where England performed better than the international average, the difference was always greater for boys than for girls;

• where England performed less well than the international average (that is, in geometry) the differential was greater for girls than boys; performance in geometry is particularly weak for English students, and even more so for English girls.

It is also salutary to note that the gender differences in the mathematics performance of the England sample were among the largest of all the countries taking part. Only Iran and Tunisia had larger and statistically significant gender differences in favour of boys. The Philippines, New Zealand and Jordan showed differences in favour of girls, but these did not reach the level of statistical significance. Within the TIMSS-R data, additional analyses were carried out on the highest attaining quartile, which showed that the percentages of boys and girls reaching the upper quartile were approximately equal. However, in Israel, Tunisia and the USA, the percentages of boys reaching the upper quartile level were significantly greater than the percentages of girls reaching it.

Figure 5.18: *A comparison of the average scale scores of the England sample in each content area of mathematics with the international average in those areas, TIMSS-R, 2000*

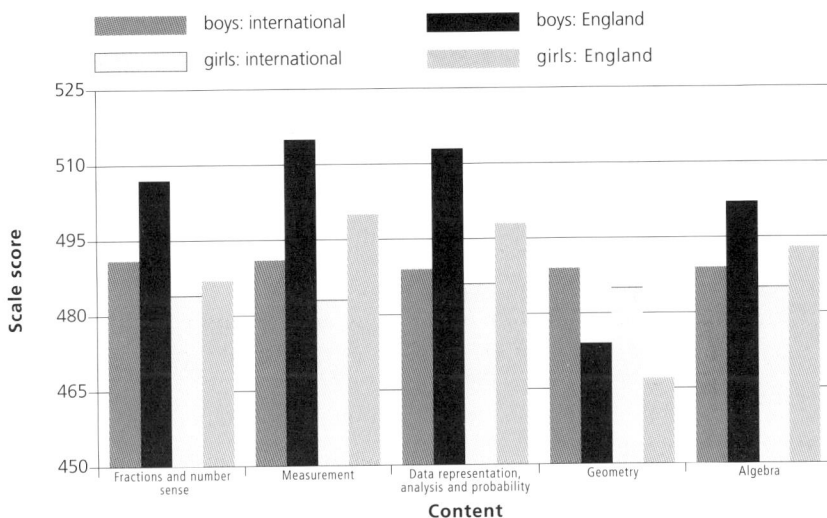

The major conclusion to be drawn here is that the TIMSS-R results are somewhat in line with our findings on the World Class Tests, although of course, the TIMSS enterprise does not seek to differentiate within the very highest levels of attainment in the subjects it covers. Nevertheless, it is important to consider the matter of content areas and their relationship to performance in the future development of the tests.

One other aspect of the content of the questions is whether or not they are set in a context. In recent years there has been much debate about setting questions in 'realistic' contexts in mathematics. Cooper and Dunne (2000) have considered 'contextual' questions in relation to social background and suggested that students from lower socio-economic groups react less well to them, and other researchers (for example, Elwood, 2000; Murphy, 1995) have shown some differential reaction to 'contexts'. This may be a factor here and is being investigated further in our data.

3. Responses and non-responses to the questions

The strong performance of boys at the higher levels of the World Class Tests in mathematics could also be explained by the way in which boys and girls chose to respond, or not respond, to the questions. To explore this, an analysis of non-responses to the questions was carried out, the results of which are presented in Figures 5.19 and 5.20 (page 80). For nine year olds and 13 year olds respectively, the graphs show the non-response pattern by gender. The columns represent the percentage of non-response to the question/test booklets and the horizontal axis shows the number of questions for which a response was not given. In the case of both the age-groups, the differences in response patterns do not reach statistical significance, although for nine year olds this was close (p=0.057). For the 13 year olds the equivalent value was (p=0.195).

Figure 5.19: *Percentage non-response rates to the questions for nine year olds*

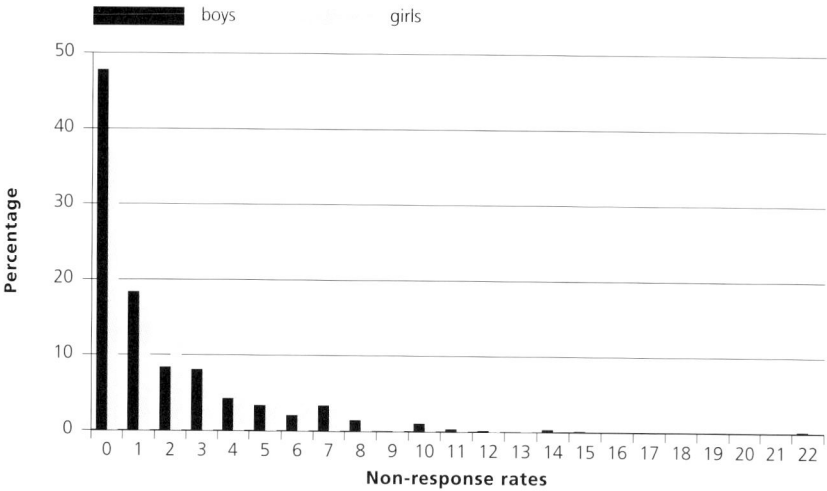

Figure 5.20: *Percentage non-response rates to the questions for 13 year olds*

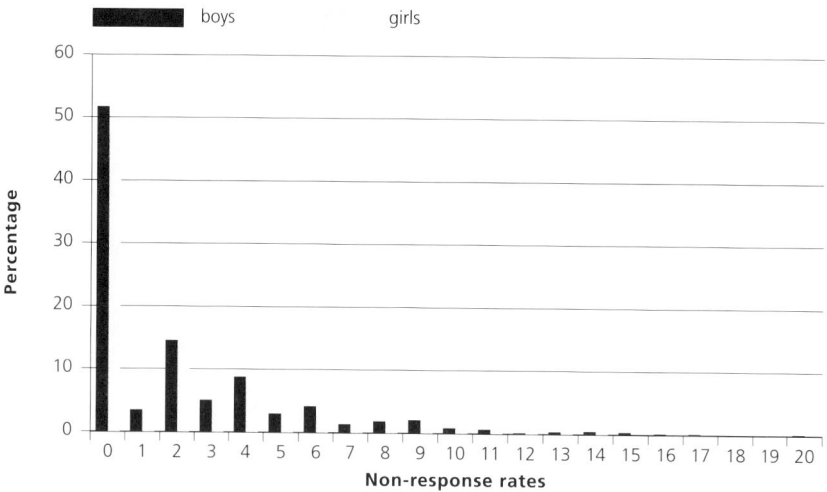

Figures 5.19 and 5.20 indicate that around 50 per cent of boys at both age-groups attempted all the questions in their booklet, whereas for the girls this was slightly lower, especially at age nine. There is therefore some evidence to suggest that the non-response rate for girls is consistently higher than for boys at age nine. This may indicate different degrees of confidence in facing some of these rather difficult and unusual mathematics questions. This would be in line with other work suggesting lower confidence and expectations for girls (Stobart *et al.*, 1992; Elwood and Murphy, 2000).

It may also be related, though less directly, to the findings on girls' responses to 'None of the above' distractors in multiple choice questions (Fraenkel, 2000).

4. Sampling effects and teacher selection strategies

It is possible, of course, that these gender effects in the World Class Tests samples are the results of particular selection strategies. The total sample came from a representative sample of schools in England and the teachers made the selection of students within their classes or schools according to clear criteria. They were asked to select the top 20 per cent of their year-groups in mathematics and also to supply us with their Teacher Assessment (TA) judgement (by national curriculum level) for each student selected. This yielded total samples for each of the two age-groups that had broadly equivalent numbers of boys and girls and for whom the TA judgements were broadly equivalent (see the earlier data in this paper). This information is given in Table 5.3, below.

Table 5.3: *The percentage of boys and girls in the samples at each Teacher Assessment (TA) level for the two age-groups*

YEAR GROUP AND TA LEVEL	% BOYS	% GIRLS
Nine year olds		
TA Level 3	14.6	14.7
TA Level 4	85.4	85.3
13 year olds		
TA Level 5/6	45.9	54.7
TA Level 7/8	54.1	45.3

The nine year olds sample proved virtually the same for boys and girls. The sample of 13 year olds, on the other hand, seems balanced in favour of boys at the higher levels. In order to test this further, analyses were carried out holding TA constant, and when this 'correction' was made, the performance advantage of boys persisted.

Of course, this may not be the whole story on selection procedures, and it is certainly an issue we are following up in our subsequent analyses. At present, a further large-scale pre-test is under way and similar analyses will be carried out to investigate further these gender issues. In particular, teachers will be asked to tell us about their student selection procedures for these tests. Given the agenda of the World Class Tests, it is important that students who may have the talent and ability should be given access to this kind of assessment, without teacher judgements potentially acting as a barrier. False negatives are as important as false positives in this context.

5. Real differences in the abilities of boys and girls?

A recent review of the relevant neurological evidence in relation to gender has been provided by Blakemore and Frith (2001), at the invitation of the national Economic and Social Research Council (ESRC) Teaching and Learning Research programme. This section of their report suggests clear differences in the structure of male and female brains (Good *et al*, 2000), but the significance of these differences is as yet poorly understood and is a matter of some dispute. However, there have been some consistent reported findings over many years that women outperform men on verbal tasks and that men seem to be better at spatial tasks. These findings may help to explain the kinds of differences reported in this paper, but the evidence is not yet sufficiently clear to make unequivocal statements about mathematical performance and differential neurological functioning.

Conclusions and implications

This chapter has shown the following, in a preliminary way.

• In England, the strong performance of girls and the under-achievement of boys in our assessment system is seen as a significant educational and political issue. The national assessment data are taken as evidence for this.

• Preliminary evidence from our work on the World Class Tests shows that, in mathematics at least, boys seem to outperform girls at the highest levels of attainment, giving some pause for thought.

• Closer inspection of the national test data in mathematics, however, serves to reinforce the kind of pattern of performance found in the World Class Tests: boys do significantly better than girls at the higher levels.

• In fact, the TIMSS-R data (Ruddock, 2000) show that in the England sample, boys' performance was sustained and slightly improved between 1995 and 1999, whilst that of girls declined in a quite marked way. This kind of information seems to be at odds with our national data, where even if girls do not outperform boys, they at least hold their own.

• There is some evidence that non-response rates to questions differ between boys and girls, but this needs further investigation.

• Performance in the World Class Tests in mathematics also shows some evidence of content effects in relation to gender, which again needs further explorations and verification.

• However, detailed analysis of individual questions where there are significant gender differences in performance reveals little by way of additional explanation.

The next key point is the wider verification of these preliminary findings in the next set of data. If the new data continues to produce these outcomes, then there are significant questions to be asked about potential gender issues in the World Class Tests in mathematics.

6 Using assessment to facilitate the development and enhancement of mathematically promising students

Linda Jensen Sheffield
Northern Kentucky University, USA

FOR MORE THAN A DECADE there has been a push to raise academic levels in the United States through standards-based initiatives, and most teachers agree that this has raised expectations for all students and helped create a more demanding curriculum (Olson, 2001a, p. 8). In mathematics, many of these initiatives followed the publication of the *Curriculum and Evaluation Standards* by the National Council of Teachers of Mathematics (NCTM, 1989). Many states moved to align their state standards with these national guidelines when they were published. In 2000, when NCTM revised the original *Standards*, following extensive review, and published the *Principles and Standards for School Mathematics* (NCTM, 2000), many states also revised their own guidelines.

Along with the development of state standards came the call for more local and district accountability. Districts and states began to develop assessment and accountability systems. Because educational decisions on issues such as curriculum, instruction and assessment are made at a state or local level, the type of testing and accountability systems used vary widely from state to state and even from district to district. All states but one (Iowa) now have content or curriculum standards in mathematics and 43 states have some type of criterion-referenced mathematics assessment aligned to these state standards (Orlofsky and Olson, 2001).

In any type of assessment and accountability system, the purpose of the assessment must be considered. One goal that is often stated for any accountability system is to hold schools and students responsible for learning at a high level. For our top students, this is may be a difficult task. Assessment is often directed at levels that

For brief notes on the US education system, please see page 128.

all students should master, and neglects those students who find the assessment items lacking any challenge. This lack of challenge in assessment is often mirrored in the general lack of attention to bright mathematics students in the classroom.

The *Agenda for Action* from the National Council of Teachers of Mathematics (NCTM, 1980) stated:

> *The student most neglected, in terms of realizing full potential, is the gifted student of mathematics. Outstanding mathematical ability is a precious societal resource, sorely needed to maintain leadership in a technological world.*

In 1995, NCTM appointed a Task Force on Promising Students. In the Task Force Report (Sheffield *et al.*, 1995), mathematical promise is described as a function of ability, motivation, belief, and experience or opportunity. None of the variables are viewed as fixed, but rather as areas that need to be developed so that mathematical success might be maximised for an increased number of promising students. This description recognises that abilities can be enhanced and developed, and acknowledges research that documents changes in the brain due to experiences. It also concedes that students are not always motivated to achieve at their highest possible levels. Popular culture in the United States may even encourage students to disguise their mathematical abilities in order to avoid negative labels. Belief in one's ability to succeed and belief in the importance of mathematical success by students, teachers, peers and parents are also recognised as important. The lack of such beliefs among some groups is acknowledged as a significant barrier to learning. The importance of the fourth variable, experience or opportunity to learn, is especially evident in international comparisons of mathematics students where research frequently finds that students in the United States are not exposed to the same high level of curriculum as students in several other countries.

If students in the United States are to perform at world-class levels, standards, expectations and assessment levels must be raised for all students, including those who are already performing in the top 5 per cent when compared to their classmates. It is not enough to say that a student is performing at the 95th percentile on some standardised United States mathematics test, if that test is not assessing performance at an international level comparable to those in the highest-performing countries. One of the purposes of assessing high mathematical standards should be to create students who are able to perform at those high levels. This has not always been the case.

Background

MATHEMATICS PERFORMANCE IN THE US IN THE LIGHT OF INTERNATIONAL COMPARISONS

Results from the Third International Mathematics and Science Study *(TIMSS)* showed that the best mathematics students in the United States are not achieving at the level of top students in other countries (see www.ustimss.msu.edu). In fourth grade, 9 per cent of US students scored above the 90th percentile worldwide on the *TIMSS* mathematics test. By eighth grade, only 5 per cent of US mathematics students tested scored above the 90th percentile. This is in contrast to countries such as Singapore, where 39 per cent of the fourth graders and 45 per cent of the eighth graders scored among the top 10 per cent of all students tested (United States Department of

Education, 1997). (In England, 7 per cent of the Year 5/fourth graders and 7 per cent of the Year 9/eighth graders scored at these levels.) At the end of secondary school, advanced mathematics and physics students in the United States scored significantly below advanced students in many other countries. Results such as these have caused several educators in the United States to be concerned about the future of our best mathematics students.

Following the *TIMSS* study, one frequently-heard analysis of the mathematics curriculum in the United States is that it is 'an inch deep and a mile wide' (Schmidt *et al*, 1996). Mathematics textbooks in the United States tend to cover large numbers of topics at a relatively shallow level and repeat the same topics for years. The type of mathematics assessment that is used can exacerbate the situation. If we only assess low-level mathematics, teachers will teach to that level. Some widely used standardised mathematics tests have been criticised for testing students' abilities to memorise facts and perform low-level computational algorithms rather than their abilities to think and reason mathematically. In May 2001, the United States Congress debated whether to introduce compulsory testing in mathematics and reading for all students every year from third grade through to eighth grade, and the question of the effects of testing became a critical one.

MATHEMATICS ASSESSMENT IN THE COMMONWEALTH OF KENTUCKY

One state that has been at the forefront of education reform, assessment and accountability is Kentucky. In 1989, the Commonwealth of Kentucky began a process of educational reform based on the belief that all students can learn at high levels. They moved to a standards-based assessment programme that set higher levels of expectations for achievement in all subject areas. All students are expected to perform at a level of 'Proficient' or above in each subject area. (Student performance in each subject area is determined to be one of four levels ranging from 'Novice' at the low end to 'Apprentice', then 'Proficient', and finally 'Distinguished' at the top of the range.) Each school has the goal of having a school-wide index that reflects an average of 'Proficient' (an index of 100 or higher) before the year 2015. No school in the state has yet reached this goal for all subject areas, although some schools have reached the goal in mathematics at some grade levels. To achieve this goal, school districts must support all students as they strive to reach higher levels and must set high expectations of distinguished levels of performance from large numbers of students. Schools will not reach their goals without a significant numbers of students reaching the distinguished level unless fewer students perform at less than proficient levels. Therefore, many schools are looking for ways to support larger numbers of students as they learn higher levels of mathematics.

Recognising that teachers will teach to the test, especially if the stakes are high, education officials in Kentucky stressed the importance of a state-wide assessment system that was closely tied to the academic expectations and Program of Studies and that required written responses to questions involving reasoning that went beyond memorised facts and algorithms.

In 2001, it was noted that changes in assessment in Kentucky (Olson, 2001b, p. 24) *had sent a clear signal to teachers that they needed to work on problem-solving in mathematics and on the written communication of mathematical ideas. Teachers also added new content to their classrooms to reflect what was on the assessments.*

In this way, the assessment was driving a positive change in the classroom toward more emphasis on problem solving and written communication of mathematical concepts.

Implementing reform in Kentucky

ACADEMIC EXPECTATIONS AND THE PROGRAM OF STUDIES

One of the first steps in implementing educational reform in Kentucky was to establish six learning goals that were aligned with the state's educational mission and philosophy. Hundreds of teachers from all grade levels and subject areas were called upon to write and revise mission statements, philosophies and goals that everyone could support. The agreed mission centred on providing an internationally superior education and love of learning for each student, based upon the philosophy that all children could learn at high levels. In addition, teachers in effective schools were found to expect a high level of achievement from all students and to align curriculum, instruction and assessment.

Before individual schools could be expected to align curriculum, instruction and assessment, the Kentucky Department of Education again called together public school teachers and the university faculty to outline specific academic expectations for each subject area. In mathematics, these academic expectations were based on the *Curriculum and Evaluation Standards* (NCTM, 1989). These state expectations have been revised and clarified periodically over the past 10 years, most notably when the new *Principles and Standards* were developed (NCTM, 2000). A Program of Studies has been developed for each subject area at each grade level so that administrators, teachers, parents and students know what topics should be learned each year. (See the Kentucky Department of Education website at www.kde.state.ky.us for more information.) The Academic Expectations and corresponding Program of Studies form the basis for all state-wide curriculum and assessment that has been developed since 1989, and most school districts in the state have aligned their own curriculum, instruction, and assessment to these standards.

Mathematics is assessed in Kentucky in Grades 3, 6 and 9 using a popular national test that allows teachers, parents, and students to compare the work of the students to national norms. This test utilises mostly multiple-choice items and is not directly correlated with state expectations. Therefore, education officials and teachers in Kentucky have found it important to use tests that are aligned with state goals and that use open response as well as multiple-choice questions. These state tests, known as the *Kentucky Core Content Tests (KCCT)* are given to students in Grades 5, 8 and 11 and are designed to be reflective of the state goals and objectives in mathematics (see www.kde.state.ky.us).

CORE CONTENT FOR ASSESSMENT

To aid teachers, students, and test developers, Core Content for Assessment has been outlined for each subject area in the years that it is assessed using state-developed tests. For mathematics, this means that there is a list of critical mathematics content outlined for Grades 5, 8 and 11. At each grade level, the content is divided into four areas: number and computation; geometry and measurement; probability and statistics; algebraic ideas. These four strands are divided into 'concepts', 'skills' and 'relationships':

• **concepts** are mathematical ideas that serve as the basis for understanding mathematics;

- **skills** are actions of mathematics;
- **relationships** connect mathematical concepts and skills within mathematics and in the real world.

An abridged version of the Core Content for Assessment for Grade 5 is shown in Tables 6.1a and 6.1b (pages 88 and 89).

Problem solving is expected to be a central focus of the mathematics program that permeates all four content strands and should provide the context in which the concepts, skills, and relationships are learned.

The *Kentucky Core Content Tests* (see www.kde.state.ky.us) are developed using the Core Content as a basis. Items are written by Kentucky teachers following state guidelines and tied to the Core Content. Each item is field-tested both using out-of-state students and as part of the regular state testing which is completed each April. (For more information see the Core Content for Assessment section on the Kentucky Department of Education website.)

OPEN RESPONSE QUESTIONS

Open response questions are a critical component of the *Kentucky Core Content Tests*. They are considered a hallmark of a 'thinking' curriculum and are designed to encourage students to integrate and apply knowledge and skills to a variety of situations. The Kentucky Department of Education has developed a manual for writing open response questions, which may be seen on the website. This was designed to help teachers incorporate open response questions into daily classroom teaching. This is another example of the state assessment system being designed to drive appropriate classroom instruction.

Previous testing had been found to focus on lower-level memorising and computation skills, and open response questions were designed to encourage students to think and reason at a higher level, thereby encouraging teachers to incorporate more of this type of questioning into everyday lessons. Open response questions should give teachers a deeper insight into students' thinking processes and their understanding of the Core Content and should help students gain a deeper understanding of the learning process. Teachers are taught to begin the design of open response items by asking themselves which of the 'big ideas' in the unit they wish students to demonstrate an ability to apply. Many of the questions are scaffolded: that is, they ask students several questions about the same situation, with each question building upon the previous one and increasing in difficulty or complexity. This is often a way to allow all students the opportunity to enter the question at an appropriate level and have some degree of success. The latter parts of these questions are frequently more difficult and are designed to challenge even the best students.

Because open response items are frequently designed to encourage students to find solutions using a variety of methods, designing a scoring guide to match each individual item becomes an important part of the development of the item itself. Teachers are encouraged to develop sample responses that are reflective of the high level of response they expect from the students. Students become an integral part of deciding upon the most exemplary responses, and are encouraged to answer a question in such a way that their responses might be used as an example for other students to follow. Student performance on open response items increases significantly as they have more experience and as they observe other students' top-quality responses. They are encouraged to critically evaluate the questions they are asked as well as their own and their peers' responses.

Table 6.1a: *Core Content for Assessment, Grade 5 mathematics – number/computation and geometry/measurement*

NUMBER/COMPUTATION	
Concepts	Whole numbers, fractions, mixed numbers, and decimals through thousandths
	The operations of addition, subtraction, multiplication, and division
	Odd and even numbers, composite and prime numbers, multiples, and factors
	Place value, expanded form, number magnitude to 100,000,000, and decimals…
	Multiple representations of numbers
Skills	Read, write, and rename whole numbers
	Add, subtract, multiply, and divide whole numbers using a variety of methods
	Add and subtract fractions with like denominators; add and subtract decimals…
	Skip-count forward and backward
	Estimate quantities of objects
	Estimate computational results using an appropriate strategy
	Use factors to determine prime and composite numbers
	Determine least common multiple
	Order and compare whole numbers and fractions
Relationships	How fractions, decimals, and whole numbers relate
	How properties are used in computation
	How the base 10 number system relates to place value
GEOMETRY/MEASUREMENT	
Concepts	Basic geometric elements and terms
	Basic two-dimensional shapes
	Basic three-dimensional shapes
	Symmetry, congruence, and similar figures
	Nonstandard and standard units of measurement
Skills	Sort objects and compare attributes
	Use symmetry to construct a geometric design
	Identify and draw basic two-dimensional shapes in different orientations
	Identify basic three-dimensional shapes by appearance
	Use nonstandard and standard units to measure weight, length, perimeter, area, and angles
	Use standard units to measure volume…, liquid capacity, money, time, and temperature
	Choose appropriate tools for specific measurement tasks
	Identify measurable attributes of an object and estimate using appropriate units…
	Use measurements to describe and compare attributes of objects
Relationships	How two-dimensional shapes are alike or different
	How three-dimensional shapes are alike or different
	How units within the same measurement system are related
	How lines of symmetry relate to shapes

Table 6.1b: *Core Content for Assessment, Grade 5 mathematics – probability/statistics and algebraic thinking*

PROBABILITY/STATISTICS	
Concepts	Mean, median, mode, and range of a set of data
	Probability of an unlikely event and likely event
	The process of using data to answer questions
Skills	Pose questions that can be answered by collecting data
	Collect, organize, and describe data
	Construct and interpret displays of data
	Interpret circle graphs
	Make predictions and draw conclusions based on data
	Find mean, median, mode, and range of a set of data
	Generate all possible outcomes in simple probability activities
	Determine the fairness of games using simple probability activities
Relationships	How data are used to draw conclusions
	How predictions can be based on probability data
	How the type of display is related to data
ALGEBRAIC THINKING	
Concepts	Functions through pictures, tables, and words
	Number sentences with a missing value or variable
	A positive coordinate system of graphing using ordered pairs
Skills	Find rules for, extend, and create patterns
	Create tables to analyse patterns/functions
	Find solutions to number sentences with a missing value
	Locate whole numbers, fractions, and decimals on a number line
	Graph ordered pairs on a positive coordinate grid
Relationships	How patterns are alike and different
	How rules involving number patterns can be explained

Abridged from: http://www.kde.state.ky.us/oapd/curric/corecontent/core_content_index_version_30.asp

SCORING GUIDES

Another of the benefits of the state testing system is that a number of items are released each year and published in both print and electronic form so that teachers around the world may use them. Not only are sample items and scoring guides released: sample student responses are also provided, with comments from scorers, so that teachers know what to look for. Many of the released items also contain instructional strategies, which will assist teachers in planning instruction that is correlated to the Academic Expectations, Core Content, and Program of Studies. Some of these may be found on the Kentucky Department of Education website.

DESCRIPTORS OF MATHEMATICAL EXPECTATIONS

As the state assessment items are developed, the teachers who are writing them attempt to design items that will elicit responses that meet high-level expectations. These expectations are spelled out for the assessment grades of five, eight and 11 with descriptions for each level of performance (Novice, Apprentice, Proficient and Distinguished). Abridged versions of the descriptors of Grade 5 Mathematical Expectations are shown in Table 6.2 (page 90).

These descriptors are designed to give teachers and students goals to strive for not only in the conceptual understanding and skills related to mathematical content, but

Table 6.2: *An abridged version of the descriptors of Grade 5 mathematical expectations*

	DISTINGUISHED	PROFICIENT	APPRENTICE	NOVICE
Skills, Concepts and Relationships	Student demonstrates **comprehensive** understanding of 5th grade skills, concepts, and relationships.	Student demonstrates understanding of 5th grade skills, concepts, and relationships.	Student demonstrates **basic or partial** understanding of 5th grade skills, concepts, and relationships.	Student demonstrates a **limited** understanding of 5th grade skills, concepts, and relationships.
Mathematical Strategies	Student **consistently** implements **appropriate** strategies.	Student implements **appropriate** strategies most of the time.	Student **attempts** to use strategies to solve problems some of the time.	Student demonstrates **limited** understanding of problems and fails to apply an appropriate strategy.
Understanding	Student demonstrates an **extensive** understanding of the problem with correct solutions.	Student demonstrates a **general** understanding of the problem with correct solutions most of the time (correct and complete, with minor computational errors possible).	Student demonstrates **basic or partial** understanding of the problem with correct solutions some of the time.	Student demonstrates **limited** understanding of the problems with incomplete or incorrect solutions.
Terminology and Representations	Student uses **appropriate and accurate** mathematical terminology and representations in a clear and concise manner.	Student uses **appropriate and accurate** mathematical terminology and/or representations effectively.	Student **attempts** to use mathematical terminology and/or representations but terminology/ representations may be unclear and/or misused.	Student **rarely or ineffectively** uses mathematical terminology and/or representations, which are appropriate for 5th grade.
Reasoning	Student demonstrates mathematical reasoning (support) in an **appropriate and consistent** manner.	Student demonstrates mathematical reasoning (support), **but may be unclear, or incomplete.**	Student demonstrates **limited or partial** mathematical reasoning (support).	Student demonstrates **inappropriate** mathematical reasoning (support is not present).

For full version, see Kentucky Department of Education (2001).

also in the areas of problem solving, use of mathematical strategies, representations, and terminology, and reasoning. Each of these areas gets progressively more complex as the grade levels increase, giving teachers and students guidelines for adding depth and complexity to mathematical problem solving and reasoning. Guidelines are also provided as to the content in the areas of number and computation; probability and statistics; geometry and measurement; and algebraic ideas. Once again, the emphasis is on aligning curriculum, assessment, and instruction with the goal of raising the level of proficiency for all students, including those who are already performing at a proficient level.

MATHEMATICS ASSESSMENT RESULTS

One persistent problem on a national and international level, as well as a state level, is the fact that mathematical performance is often negatively correlated with the level of poverty of the students in the sample. Results from the *TIMSS-R* 1999 Benchmarking Study showed that while United States school districts at the high end of the continuum in mathematics, such as the Naperville School District and the First in the World Consortium (both relatively wealthy school districts in Illinois), scored similarly to Hong Kong and Japan, urban districts with high percentages of students from low-income families and minorities performed similarly to lower-performing countries in TIMSS (such as Turkey, Jordan and Iran). Results from *TIMSS-R* tend to support research that shows that students in urban districts often attend schools that have a less challenging curriculum and fewer resources and come from homes that also have fewer educational resources. (For details see http://nces.ed.gov/TIMSS/timss-r/benchmark.asp)

Some schools in Kentucky with high poverty rates seem able to break this cycle, however. Susan Weston (2000a, b and c), who prepared the report *Performance and Poverty*, noted that the weakest performance on state tests comes from schools with some poverty, but not the highest levels of poverty. Some schools with poverty rates among the highest 10 per cent in the state had average assessment scores also in the top 10 per cent of the state. Principals and teachers of these schools reported that they strongly believed that all students could learn at high levels, and they accepted no excuses for low levels of achievement. Table 6.3 (page 92) shows the top five and bottom five schools at Grade 5 based upon mathematics scores from the 1999 and 2000 *Kentucky Core Content Test*.

The percentage of students receiving free and reduced lunch is the best available indicator of the poverty rate. The greater the percentage of these students, the greater the rate of poverty. Note that while there is not a perfect correlation between poverty rate and mathematics scores, there remains a strong link between the two.

At all grade levels, the top performing schools have around half or more of their students performing at the distinguished level and top schools at the fifth and eighth grade levels have fewer than one-fifth of their students performing below the proficient level. Students in the poorest performing schools do not have these same opportunities. In these schools, one per cent or fewer of the students are scoring at the distinguished level while 90 per cent or more score below the proficient level. It is hard to know how many students in these schools could have become outstanding mathematicians or scientists but were never given the opportunity to learn high-level mathematics. These schools are now receiving assistance from the state and federal government in an effort to raise expectations and opportunities, but progress is sometimes agonisingly slow. Additional information on all school scores in all subject areas can be found on the Kentucky Department of Education website.

Table 6.3: *Top five and bottom five schools at Grade 5 in mathematics*

SCHOOL DISTRICT	SCHOOL	99 MATH INDEX	99 N NOVICE	99 AP APPREN.	99 PR PROFIC.	99 D DISTING	00 MATH INDEX	00 N NOVICE	00 AP APPREN.	00 PR PROFIC.	00 D DISTING.	FREE/REDUCED LUNCH %
OC	LE	105.4875	2	28	16	44	121.9958	2	12	19	67	14
AI	APS	111.7400	2	20	26	52	119.314	0	17	24	59	0
OC	GE	108.0490	1	32	22	46	118.268	6	10	28	57	3
FTI	JE	113.6360	0	29	15	56	108.6331	2	28	19	49	3
FC	ME	103.2400	0	33	24	43	106.7796	2	22	35	41	12
State Average		64.0301	24	55	10	11	67.0614	21	54	13	12	55
HC	VE	32.8667	52	47	0	0	33.4871	58	43	0	0	97
CI	FDE	23.1316	71	25	1	1	33.1491	64	34	2	0	91
KC	AE	46.4841	35	62	3	0	30.906	72	27	0	0	94
KC	DE	26.9147	73	26	0	0	30.2009	63	37	0	0	100
KTC	BCE	17.4871	94	6	0	0	27.68	82	28	0	0	92

Abridged from 1999–2000 Kentucky Core Content Tests mathematics data.

RECOMMENDATIONS

In spite of the progress made during the last 10 years in raising the level of mathematics achievement in Kentucky, much work continues to be needed. Research has shown that when administrators, teachers, parents and students themselves have high expectations of success, when schools offer a challenging curriculum matched to state and national goals; when instruction focuses on problem solving, reasoning, and communication; and when assessment is designed to drive focused, complex, and interesting instruction, students can and will succeed at high levels. This is true of students from all racial and ethnic backgrounds and socio-economic groups. Progress is not easy and success may not be swift, but the goals are attainable if we stay focused on the development and enhancement of all students' mathematical promise.

Issues Arising from Assessment

Overview

Gordon Stobart

University of London Institute of Education, London, UK

The previous parts of this book have as their main themes the assessment of problem-solving and of mathematics. Part III raises the broader issues of how we define and identify the 'gifted and talented'; it also examines the role of testing in the identification process.

The three papers draw on international experience in this area. In Chapter 7, E. Jean Gubbins (of the National Research Center on the Gifted and Talented, University of Connecticut, USA) provides a thought-provoking summary of how intelligence and giftedness have often, historically, been controversial concepts. She also raises the critical question of the purposes of developing schemes of assessment for the gifted and talented. Ron Casey and Valsa Koshy (of the Brunel Able Children's Education Centre, Brunel University, UK) focus particularly on how we might better identify 'submerged talent', particularly in deprived areas, and the role that World Class Tests might play in this. The third contribution is from Rosalind Elder (of the Gifted Education Research, Resource and Information Centre, Sydney, Australia). The primary purpose of the work she reports is seen as differentiating among students who are performing at the top of grade-related scales to determine who are the academically gifted.

We probably all operate with implicit understandings of what a 'gifted and talented' individual may be like. However, as E. Jean Gubbins shows, even a working definition will often prove contentious. One issue here is how far beyond 'academic potential' we are prepared to look. For example, the work of Howard Gardner (1983) on multiple intelligences, has challenged any narrow views of intelligence. A time-honoured response is to determine the proportion of the cohort who will be classified as 'gifted' (for example, the top 5 per cent). In Chapter 8, Ron Casey and Valsa Koshy illustrate some of the problems of this approach at school or regional level, given that giftedness may not be evenly distributed. The programme that Rosalind Elder outlines in Chapter 9, the Australian Primary Talent Search, seeks to differentiate within the group of primary pupils who have been identified as talented by a variety of conventional measures.

One of the key themes of these chapters is 'who are we trying to identify as gifted and talented?' The Australian Primary Talent Search aims to identify those children who are already seen as academically gifted to help them get a better education than they might otherwise have. This contrasts with the American and English approaches, which are more concerned with identifying *latent* and *emergent* talent (Chapter 7) or *submerged* talent (Chapter 8) than with *manifest* talent. The issue then becomes what *type* of assessment will search out those students whose circumstances mean they may not be picked up through conventional assessments.

This also links to purpose. World Class Tests can be used in a formative way, which provides insight into pupils' reasoning and provides teachers with feedback that may lead to revised expectations. Ron Casey and Valsa Koshy provide a case study of just such a process. This formative purpose, which enriches teaching and learning, is central. My own agenda is to ensure that this remains the case and to monitor managerial pressures to use the tests and their results for competitive purposes.

7 Assessing gifted and talented children: to what end?

E. Jean Gubbins
The National Research Center on the Gifted and Talented, University of Connecticut, USA

Introduction

IT IS ALMOST IMPOSSIBLE to think of the phrase 'gifted and talented' without thinking about assessment. This link was established centuries ago as a result of asking questions about the power, strength, cunning or potential leadership among society's minions. Of course, each society developed its own vision of 'gifted and talented.' What did the society honour? What did the society need? How were people's abilities recognised and nurtured? How did this vision affect the society's culture, productivity and cohesiveness and its social, economic and political structures? It is interesting to note that, in the twenty-first century, we are still debating these same questions.

Moving from centuries ago to 100 years ago, the biggest impact on how such questions were posed or answered was made by the testing movement in the 1900s. People on both sides of the Atlantic tried to establish ways to assess people. In France, advertisements existed in 'billboard fashion', calling for assessment of abilities in anthropometric laboratories. What could we learn about how the human brain functions? There were so many mysteries to uncover about human abilities and potentials. As tasks or test items were developed, more and more data were available for interpretation, indicating that people responded in different ways. What did the differences mean? Were these differences stable over time? Did these differences predict future behaviour? Such questions have still not been resolved to the total satisfaction of everyone. We still need to think about assessment and we need to understand its impact.

There are many reasons why people want to assess other people and themselves. Assessment has multiple purposes, as
- a source of knowledge;
- a process;
- an end state.

For brief notes on the US education system, please see page 128.

Each of these purposes will be introduced briefly to underline the complexities of assessment as a specialised field of gathering data that helps us to learn more about how people function and think.

ASSESSMENT AS A SOURCE OF KNOWLEDGE

As a source of knowledge, assessment techniques include tests, interviews, portfolios, performances, observations, projects or competitions. These techniques, individually or collectively, provide carefully gathered information to help us understand how people function in comparison to others, or even to oneself, during a prior assessment opportunity. Solving complex real-world problems, reflecting on what we can do and what we can do well, and engaging in well-defined tasks are examples of formal and informal assessment. Three examples follow.

Solving real-world problems

Imagine working in a laboratory and trying to resolve the intricacies of a disease that was rampant in the United States in the 1950s. During hot, summer days, people flocked to local lakes or ponds. The joy of frolicking in the cool water soon waned, however, as people became ill. Later, the illness was identified as polio, which caused paralysis. The fear of contracting polio was a summer reality. Jonas Salk recognised the problem, tried to unravel its intricacies, and spent almost all of his time experimenting with solutions that did not work. As each potential solution to polio was assessed and eliminated, it was evident that his knowledge of the disease expanded, but its intricacies remained elusive for quite a while. His discovery of the polio vaccine was an incredible accomplishment and an example of how real-world problems may be solved.

Reflecting on what we can do well

When you hear the name Paul Gauguin, what vision comes to mind? Do you think about tropical islands with large expanses of brightly-coloured foliage and flowers? Are people in native dress luxuriating in the tranquil environment? Or do you see the floor of a trading market similar to Wall Street in New York or the Tokyo Stock Exchange? Well, before Paul Gauguin became a famous painter, he struggled as a stockbroker. His artistic abilities were of a different calibre to his financial trading skills: he was not as gifted in both fields.

Engaging in well-defined tasks

Melony and her middle school friends heard that a local school was having trouble with water quality. They wondered if they could find out why the water was contaminated. They talked with the principal, and she suggested that they develop a plan to identify the possible source of contamination. The students contacted a local university by e-mail, and they asked if someone would help them test the local water. At first, the university professor who responded to the e-mail was reluctant. However, when she read the students' plan, she realised how committed they were to the project. The middle school students continued their communication with the professor and together, through specific, well-defined tasks, they developed a systematic approach to uncover the source of contamination.

Assessment as a source of knowledge may take various directions as information is acquired and verified. We learn, we question and, perhaps, start again.

ASSESSMENT AS A PROCESS

Assessment is also a process or series of actions directed toward a particular aim. Three basic questions should guide this process:

• What do we want to know?
• Why do we want to know the information?
• How will the information be used?

As a process, assessment must have an aim or a goal. If we want information about student performance, we need to understand the reasons why we need the data. Otherwise, the process will be aimless. Student performance is at the heart of all educational expectations: what do we want students to know, understand and do? This question is not always easy to answer, but it must be central to any assessment technique. Otherwise, we end up collecting data that are neither timely nor appropriate. Of course, before we start any data collection process, we have to think carefully through several questions. How will the information be used? Will the assessment process help us to guide, understand and improve student learning?

ASSESSMENT AS AN END STATE

Assessment is often viewed as something that occurs after information is presented and practised. We learn knowledge, concepts, skills, or attitudes and then assessment techniques provide documentation of the extent to which we understand, and possibly apply, this learning. This purpose of assessment as an end state strengthens accountability. Essentially, did students 'know it, understand it and use it?' How well did each student 'know it, understand it and use it?' The end state helps us understand students' needs, provides information to parents, educators or policy makers, and promotes better instruction. If students do not seem to know it, understand it, or use it, we must examine instructional techniques, curricular objectives, as well as initial expectations.

Given the complexities of assessment, it is important for educators to understand how it can be used productively. Viewing the purposes of assessment as a source of knowledge, process and an end state ensures that we are planning, designing, and implementing techniques that improve educational opportunities for young people. Early theorists and researchers wanted to learn more about human behaviours and potentials. Why did some people learn complex tasks easily? Why did other people struggle with easy tasks? What accounted for these differences? How could these differences be measured? In an effort to gain knowledge about differences in performance, researchers wanted to assess children of varying abilities.

Understanding intelligence

The importance of assessment as a 'source of knowledge' explains the quest for understanding intelligence in the early 1800s. Sir Francis Galton (1822–1911) was one person who was on this quest. His research was influenced by the findings of his cousin Charles Darwin. Galton believed that the senses (vision, hearing, smell and touch) distinguished one person from another. He attributed these differences to heredity. Galton's research and thinking were documented in his seminal work entitled

Hereditary Genius (Galton, 1869). Was heredity the only influence on abilities?

One distinguished psychologist was highly influenced by the works of Galton. Charles Spearman, famous British psychologist, is credited as 'the first systematic psychometrician and the father of what is known today as classical test theory' (Sternberg, 1994, p.1008). As a classical theorist in the study of human mental ability, 'he discovered g, the general factor in the correlations among all complex tests' (Sternberg, 1994, p.1008).

Researchers in France, Alfred Binet (1857–1911) and Theodore Simon (1873–1961), were challenged by their government to devise a way to assess children's abilities. They experimented with reaction time, sounds, physical strength and colours. The researchers could not discern major differences among children. As they measured other characteristics, such as memory, comprehension, and reasoning, they recognised varying levels of performance: the Binet–Simon intelligence tests were born.

The work of Alfred Binet and Theodore Simon was noticed in America. Lewis Terman (1877–1956) launched his research career by asking questions about the skills and abilities of students with disabilities and students with advanced skills for their age. He modified the Binet–Simon tests and created the *Stanford–Binet Intelligence Scale* (Terman, 1916). Terman (1925) defined intelligence as the 'top 1 per cent in general intellectual ability, as measured by the *Stanford–Binet Intelligence Scale* or a comparable instrument' (p.43).

By design, Terman's definition of intelligence applied to a limited number of people. The logic of 'intelligence is what the test measures' took hold with a lot of people. Somehow, the objectivity of test questions of increasing difficulty gave people the notion that abilities could be quantified easily. With such quantification, however, people still wondered about varying levels of performance among children and adults.

As the field of assessment gained attention, individual intelligence tests still provided the most detailed look at the performance of one person at a time. However, more information about people's abilities was desired in less time and in large groups. Assessment practices were spurred on by the United States government's interest in assessing military recruits, using group intelligence tests developed by Terman and colleagues. The assessment field became an industry closely tied to government and educational purposes. Large-scale group assessments of children became common practice.

DEFINITIONS OF GIFTED AND TALENTED

In 1970, the Congress of the United States commissioned a study about gifted and talented children and their educational opportunities. Sidney P. Marland, US Commissioner of Education, was charged with this responsibility. The advisory committee crafted the following definition:

> *Gifted and talented children are those identified by professionally qualified persons who by virtue of outstanding abilities are capable of high performance. These are children who require differentiated educational programs and services beyond those normally provided by the regular school program in order to realise their contributions to self and society.*
>
> *Children capable of high performance include those with demonstrated achievement and/or potential in any of the following areas, singly or in combination:*
>
> 1. *general intellectual ability;*
> 2. *specific academic aptitude;*

3. *creative or productive thinking;*
4. *leadership ability;*
5. *visual and performing arts;*
6. *psychomotor ability.**

(Marland, 1972, p.2)

[*Note: in 1978, psychomotor ability was eliminated from the definition.]

The advisory committee did not elaborate on how to interpret each of the six areas. However, they did comment on the minimum number of students who would most likely be deemed gifted and talented. They addressed briefly the composition of the team members who should be responsible for determining the classification. In the Education of the Gifted and Talented, Report to the Congress of the United States by the US Commissioner of Education (Marland, 1972), the advisory committee commented:

> *It can be assumed that utilization of these criteria for identification of the gifted and talented will encompass a minimum of 3 to 5 per cent of the school population.*
>
> *Evidence of gifted and talented abilities may be determined by a multiplicity of ways. These procedures should include objective measures and professional evaluation measures which are essential components of identification.*
>
> *Professionally qualified persons include such individuals as teachers, administrators, school psychologists, counselors, curriculum specialists, artists, musicians, and others with special training who are also qualified to appraise pupils' special competencies. (p.3)*

The impetus for this commissioned study was a desire to find out why special educational opportunities were appropriate and necessary to nurture, guide, and challenge the abilities and talents of young people. How could educators ensure the development of talent? The results of the study confirmed,

> *Many talented children underachieve, performing far less than their intellectual potential might suggest. We are increasingly being stripped of the comfortable notion that a bright mind will make its own way. On the contrary, intellectual and creative talent cannot survive educational neglect and apathy.*

(Marland, 1972, p.9)

The idea of gifted and talented children trying to survive educational neglect and apathy was a particularly strong argument. The commissioned study also focused attention on the loss of talent among minority groups. The report stated: 'This loss is particularly evident in the minority groups who have in both social and educational environments every configuration calculated to stifle potential talent' (Marland, 1972, p.9).

RENZULLI'S CONCEPTION OF GIFTEDNESS

Joseph S. Renzulli of the University of Connecticut was a member of Marland's advisory committee, and he, too, wondered about the loss of human potential among special populations who may not be as advantaged. He was also concerned about the population of school children, in general, whose abilities and talents may not be challenged (Renzulli, 1971, 1973). Renzulli outlined his thoughts about definitions of gifted and talented children and accompanying assessment procedures. He looked at various definitions throughout the twentieth century, and conducted an extensive literature review on 'What makes giftedness?' He recognised that tests may be powerful tools to uncover or measure talent, but they may not be perfect predictors of talent. As assessment tools, tests provided knowledge that we may or may not have from other techniques, but there were many cases where the future productivity or accomplishments of an individual were unpredictable. The phrase 'gifted and talented' became a label and an assumption about how a person should perform in school. What other factors, within the cultural, social, and economic contexts influence or enhance academic prowess, as well as creative productivity? Renzulli (1978) offered a broadened definition of gifted and talented and depicted it as a Venn diagram with a shaded portion where the three traits of giftedness come together to signify creative productivity:

> *Giftedness consists of an interaction among three basic clusters of human traits – these clusters being above-average general abilities, high levels of task commitment, and high levels of creativity. Gifted and talented children are those possessing or capable of developing this composite set of traits and applying them to any potentially valuable area of human performance. Children who manifest or are capable of developing an interaction among the three clusters, require a wide variety of educational opportunities and services that are not ordinarily provided through regular instructional programs. (p.6)*

Developing this broadened definition of giftedness and trying to influence researchers, psychologists, and educators met with a great deal of opposition. Major journals, specialising in publications on gifted and talented children and adults, did not accept his article for publication. Contemporary psychologists, educational psychologists, and theorists challenged the liberal perspective. The application of above average ability, task commitment, and creativity to various performance areas (for example, mathematics, music, statistics, history, or journalism) was not a welcomed research-based conception of giftedness (Renzulli, 1988). In reality, many people maintained that it was more parsimonious to assess a person's abilities and talents with an individual intelligence test and derive a score that signified 'gifted,' according to test developers.

GARDNER'S DEFINITION OF INTELLIGENCE

Over the next few years, people all over the world contemplated intelligence and giftedness. Howard Gardner, of Harvard University and Boston University School of Medicine, started his own journey, spurred on by a commission from the Bernard van Leer Foundation of the Netherlands. The foundation was eager to showcase what we really know about human potential. The Bernard van Leer Foundation was interested in supporting educational interventions to benefit people who may not be as advantaged due to social or economic circumstances. Gardner was particularly suited to this challenge. He conducted research on two special populations: children who were gifted in art and adults with stroke-induced brain malfunction. His research results forced him to rethink commonly accepted views of intelligence and its subsequent measurement. In 1983, Gardner's book *Frames of Mind: The Theory of Multiple Intelligences* was published. In this book, he presents the extant literature, 'ensuring that a human intelligence must be genuinely useful and important, at least in certain cultural settings' (Gardner, 1983, p.61). As Gardner contemplated human abilities that would meet specific criteria to move discussions about human abilities and potentials beyond traditional emphases on linguistic and mathematics abilities, he noted:

> *To my mind, a human intellectual competence must entail a set of skills of problem solving – enabling the individual to* resolve genuine problems or difficulties *that he or she*

encounters and, when appropriate, to create an effective product – and must also entail the potential for finding or creating problems – *thereby laying the groundwork for the acquisition of new knowledge. (pp.60–61) [Emphasis as in original.]*

Gardner's theory of human abilities or potentials covered the following areas: linguistic intelligence, musical intelligence, logical-mathematical intelligence, spatial intelligence, bodily-kinesthetic intelligence, interpersonal intelligence and intrapersonal intelligence. Several of these intelligences may be overlooked in educational settings. By offering a new theory of human potentials, Gardner re-energised the scientific, educational and measurement discussions among researchers, educators and policy makers. They praised *Frames of Mind: The Theory of Multiple Intelligences*. W. D. Wall, University of London, stated: 'Bound to be, seminal…in the way the writings of Galton and Spearman [were]' (Gardner, 1983, book jacket).

STERNBERG'S VIEW OF INTELLIGENCE

While Howard Gardner was researching views of intelligence in various cultures and within historical contexts, Robert J. Sternberg at Yale University thought about the candidates for graduate school that he encountered through the admissions process. He reflected on his own personal experiences of taking IQ tests, reviewed his summer work experiences after high school as a research assistant at Psychological Corporation and Educational Testing Service (two major US testing companies) and studied the psychological and assessment literature.

Sternberg wondered what we were really learning about bright people as we studied test scores, grades and predicted versus actual school performance. In the early years of his developing theory, Sternberg used short scenarios to illustrate his Triarchic Theory of Intelligence (Sternberg, 1985). He described three hypothetical students who applied to the graduate psychology programme at Yale University: Alice, Barbara, and Celia. Alice's application for graduate school would sail through an admissions committee. We all know people like Alice: great test scores, high grades, and excellent recommendation letters. Alice typifies someone with high level 'analytical intelligence.' Barbara's grades were not great; test scores were not great. However, recommendation letters were outstanding. People praised her early research and creativity. Her accomplishments exemplified 'creative intelligence.' Celia's grades, test scores, and recommendation letters were good, not outstanding. Her early graduate work was fine. However, she understood the type of contributions that would make a difference for future job prospects. She was 'street smart'; tests told us very little about Celia. Celia had 'practical intelligence' (Trotter, 1986).

These brief scenarios illustrate how assessing bright students is not an easy task. Potential graduate students applying to Yale University are all strong academically. Assessment test results may have different patterns, but the real distinguishing factors become more evident as graduate students pursue their own research. The process of designing, developing, and implementing an original research study was actually the real assessment of skills and abilities.

Since 1985, Sternberg has tested his Triarchic Theory of Intelligence with populations all over the world to ensure its appropriateness and applicability to other cultures. Results of multiple studies revealed that 'successful intelligence is one's ability purposively to adapt, shape, and select environments so as to accomplish one's goals and those of one's culture' (Sternberg, 2000, p.44). Essentially, to understand and maximise the abilities and talents of young people, we must go beyond a strict reliance on IQ tests and consider a focus on successful intelligence, which capitalises on analytical, creative, and practical abilities.

The assessment toolbox today

Have we come a long way in assessing gifted and talented children? Definitions of intelligence and giftedness may be broader now than they were in the early 1900s. The most current federal definition offered by the United States Department of Education is as follows:

> *Children and youth with outstanding talent perform or show the potential for performing at remarkably high levels of accomplishment when compared with others of their age, experience, and environment.*
>
> *These children and youth exhibit high performance capability in intellectual, creative, and/or artistic areas, possess an unusual leadership capacity, or excel in specific academic fields. They require services or activities not ordinarily provided by the schools.*
>
> *Outstanding talents are present in children and youth from all cultural groups, across all economic strata, and in all areas of human endeavor.*
>
> *(United States Department of Education, 1993, p.26)*

As you can see, this definition contains some phrases that are quite similar to the one proposed by Marland (1972). Both definitions refer to the need for services not ordinarily provided by schools. Both definitions note multiple areas of gifts and talents: academic, intellectual, creative, artistic and leadership skills. As opposed to the 1972 definition, the most recent federal definition does not include any reference to the percentage of students who would be deemed gifted and talented. The last sentence in the 1993 definition is probably the most critical statement, and it must be acknowledged repeatedly until the assessment of gifts and talents operates from this perspective. We cannot entertain or tolerate the sentiment that there are no gifted and talented children in a school, as was maintained by several administrators who were surveyed as part of the Marland study.

Since 1990, The National Research Center on the Gifted and Talented, federally funded research and development consortium (University of Connecticut, University of Virginia, Yale University), has conducted quantitative and qualitative studies, focusing on many issues related to identification and assessment. Archambault *et al.* (1993, p.50) conducted a large-scale survey of teachers' classroom practices in Grades 3 and 4 across the United States. As part of the demographic data about survey respondents and school districts, they gathered data on the assessment methods used in public schools (see Table 7.1, opposite).

The list shown in Table 7.1 represents an extensive assessment toolbox. Selecting or creating assessment methods should only proceed when educators have studied various conceptions of intelligence and giftedness and determine their beliefs in expectations of children.

'Remember the children' should be the phrase that guides the process of assessing and nurturing latent, emergent, and manifest abilities. Some children's advanced abilities are obvious, especially if they are precocious readers (Jackson and Roller, 1993) or they have a deep understanding of mathematical concepts

Table 7.1: *Assessment methods used in US public schools at Grades 3 and 4 (Archambault et al., 1993)*

ASSESSMENT METHODS	% OF RESPONDENTS USING EACH METHOD
Achievement tests	79
IQ tests	72
Teacher nomination	70
Teacher rating scale	57
School grades	45
Parent nomination	44
Creativity tests	20
Student products/portfolios	17
Student self-nomination	9
Peer nomination	4

Note: respondents selected as many methods as applied; therefore, totals do not equal 100 per cent.

(Waxman *et al.*, 1996). For example, a three year old starts asking questions about letters of the alphabet that always grab his attention. He will find an alphabet book among all his toys and seek out anyone within his viewing range to read it to him over and over again. He memorises each page and recites short poems about letters as someone points to the page. Before too long, he points to words in other books without prompting and says them repeatedly. Words become more and more familiar due to his constant questions. Soon this three year old will be reading short sentences.

In mathematics, some children become fascinated with coins, calendars, and clocks at an early age. As a two year old, Brent stared at a large grandfather clock in the library. He listened very carefully to the chimes. He always wanted to hold his sister's watch from Disney World. She finally gave it to him, and he wore it all day long. He would run into the library when he heard the chimes and then he would stare at his watch. He finally made a connection to the number of chimes and the actual time. He continued to be fascinated by numbers and would always ask, 'What do they mean?'

Other children need to be exposed to multiple opportunities to explore their environment, experience the wonders of nature or work with real-world problems that do not have readily available answers. Multiple opportunities to enrich their home environments and the tapestry of the curriculum may uncover some *latent* abilities and talents. In essence, how do we really know what children can do if they never had the opportunity to explore their world widely? Still other children's abilities and talents are *emergent*. They are just beginning to become *manifest*, to be noticed by others, and they need attention to fully emerge.

A brief analogy from the plant world illustrates this point. Imagine that you filled three small containers with soil and planted a couple of bean seeds in each one. You know the germination time. After about a week, you dig up the seeds in one container and notice how the seed is changing: the cotyledon is forming below the surface (*latent*). You wait another week and the plant has broken through the soil surface: it is partially visible (*emergent*). You watch the growth of the plant every day to learn more about the growing cycle. You nurture the plants by choosing a sunny location and watering the containers, as needed. When the bean plants are mature, you reap the benefits (*manifest*).

Mary Frasier of the University of Georgia (Athens, GA, USA) developed the *Frasier Talent Assessment Profile* (Frasier *et al*, 1995) as a case study format to document, understand and assess students' abilities and talents. The assessment profile requires information from multiple assessment methods to ensure the children's needs are being addressed. The last page of the profile form includes a simple diagram that prompts assessors to 'remember the child' and consider his/her needs; this is reproduced in Figure 7.1.

Figure 7.1: *Diagram from the Frasier Talent Assessment Profile (Frasier et al., 1995)*

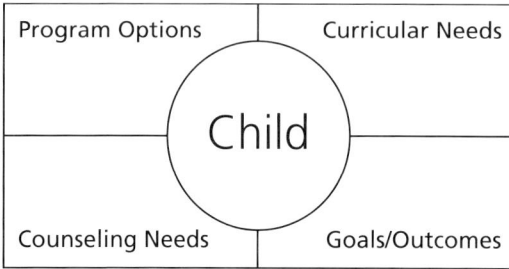

```
Program Options          Curricular Needs


              Child


Counseling Needs         Goals/Outcomes
```

Assessing gifted and talented children: the end is the beginning

As societies raise questions about human abilities and talents, their values are also tested. In 2001, people all over the world are still asking questions that were posed at the beginning of this chapter:
- What gifts and talents does society honour?
- What does the society need?
- How are people's abilities recognised and nurtured?
- How does society's vision of gifted and talented children and adults affect its culture, productivity, cohesiveness and social, economic, and political structures?

How would you respond to the above questions? As you think about your responses, you are coming to a conclusion. Assessing gifted and talented: to what end? We *respond* to talents and abilities that are *already obvious* in young people. We must also *nurture* many kinds of talents in as many people as possible. This journey will also help you reflect on your own unique abilities and talents.

The work reported herein was supported under the Educational Research and Development Centers Program PR/Award Number: R206R000001, as administered by the Office of Educational Research and Improvement, US Department of Education.

The findings and opinions expressed in this report do not necessarily reflect the positions or policies of the National Institute on the Education of At-Risk Students, the Office of Educational Research and Improvement, or the US Department of Education. Endorsement by the Federal Government should not be assumed.

8 Submerged talent and world class recognition

Ron Casey and Valsa Koshy

Brunel Able Children's Education Centre, Brunel University, Twickenham, UK

THIS PAPER EXPLORES how an education strategy yielding high performance in problem solving and mathematics can contribute significantly to endogenous growth and promote social inclusion. For World Class Tests to become an international benchmark for problem solving and mathematical performance, governments will need to share a belief that high performance in such tests correlates with future enhancement of endogenous economic growth and social inclusion.

A case study of an education programme, offered by the Brunel Able Children's Education Centre (BACE) at Brunel University to a selected group of gifted and talented children from an inner-city area suggests cognitive and social parameters for a model of education strategy which could reveal submerged talent in inner-city areas. The case study highlights the fact that the problem solving and mathematical abilities of these children have been submerged by deprivation, not eradicated by it. The findings of the case study are presented so as to argue the viability of:

- the 'gifted and talented' strand of the *Excellence in Cities* initiative (DfEE, 1999) contributing to endogenous economic growth and social inclusion (for further details, please see Appendix 1, page 127);
- high performance in the World Class Tests in problem solving and mathematics providing a two-stage national benchmark;
- the World Class Tests providing an international benchmark of performance where other governments could take the high performance into account when monitoring national education policies.

This paper outlines the ways in which the World Class Tests could be used for the purpose of talent search in inner-city areas and how they could contribute to the professional development of teachers in aspects of provision for the gifted and talented.

For brief notes on the UK education system, please see page 127.

105

Introduction

In September 2001 the United Nations General Assembly will convene a Special Session on Children. Its purpose is to agree a plan of action to ensure the realisation of the rights of every child enshrined in the Convention on the Rights of the Child, adopted in 1989. The world's top 10 per cent of the ability range of children are an integral part of the world's children: they too have rights.

A fundamental concern of the special session will, no doubt, be the measure that UNICEF regards as the primary indicator within each country of the well-being of its children: the under-five mortality rate measure U5MR. This measure indicates the probability of a child dying between birth and five years of age, expressed per 1000 live births. Early trialling of the World Class Tests may not be a priority in those countries where the probability is high.

However, 29 of the countries that the UN assigns to the category of 'industrial' have U5MR measures of less than 10. This paper explores the possibility and plausibility of the World Class Tests in problem solving and mathematics making a contribution to safeguarding the rights of the portion of the world's top 10 per cent of children residing in these 29 countries. It would not be unreasonable to append to the list countries such as Singapore, which have a low U5MR and consistent high performance in international comparative tests.

As a tentative initial support of such a consideration of World Class Tests, note should be taken of Kofi Annan, seventh Secretary-General of the United Nations, in his Foreword to 'The State of the World's Children 2001' (UNICEF, 2001). Referring to one of the three desired outcomes of the special session held in New York in September 2001, he stipulated that '... every child should have the opportunities to develop his or her full potential and contribute to society in meaningful ways'.

This paper draws attention to the possible existence of submerged talent, indicating that some children are being denied the opportunity to develop their full potential. Those found to perform sufficiently well in World Class Tests to rank them in the top 10 per cent can surely contribute to society in meaningful ways. Children within the submerged talent category who are also within the top 10 per cent would make further meaningful contributions to society – particularly in the form of innovation and technical knowledge, which is the essence of endogenous economic growth.

An educational initiative within the United Kingdom

Within the UN category of 'industrialised countries' are all seven leading industrialised nations of the world – the Group of Seven (G7). The United Kingdom is a member of G7. Yet, with its *Excellence in Cities* strand of education policy (DfEE, 1999), the Labour government has recognised that academic achievement in inner cities is significantly poorer, as measured by the percentage of children gaining five or more A to C grades at GCSE/GNVQ as compared to that of children living elsewhere in the UK.

The *Excellence in Cities* document (page 21) declares that:
Secondary schools will be expected to develop a distinct teaching and learning programme for their most able five to ten per cent of pupils.

Further, it announces that (page 27):

New World Class Tests (initially in mathematics and problem solving) will be calibrated against the performance of the best ten per cent in the highest performing countries.

Such World Class Tests are now being developed. It is assumed that they are norm-referenced. What has been under consideration within the Brunel Able Children's Education (BACE) centre, which places a major emphasis on the education of high ability students in inner-city areas, is what role the World Class Tests may have in the pursuit and development of higher ability within areas of relative deprivation.

The findings reported in this chapter relate to two Local Education Authority (LEA) districts in England. According to the Index of Local Deprivation produced by the UK Department of Environment Transport and Regions (DETR), one of them ranks among the first 12 and the other below the 150th. These rankings are based on the district level scores, of which DETR (1998) states (page 8):

The key advantage of the district level scores, which measure deprivation across the whole local authority district, is that they are based on a large number of indicators (12) many of which have been updated to 1996 or 1997.

This provides sufficient justification for accepting the rankings of the two LEAs as overall indicators, even though just two of the indicators refer to education. The case study authority ranked within the first 12 is well within the geographical area of underachievement referred to in the *Excellence in Cities* document. The other LEA is well within the geographical area of relative affluence and is therefore beyond the present concern of the initiative.

The comparative performance of the children taking World Class Tests in problem solving and mathematics, downloaded from the internet, will – it is hoped – highlight the practical implications of procedures designed to engage children – particularly those from areas of relative deprivation. As members of the BACE team deal with parents and teachers, the logic of the test-taking procedures also needs to be considered; although it is accepted that the design and content of the tests are beyond the remit of the centre staff.

THE LOGIC OF THE WORLD CLASS TESTS
Normal distributions

The target group of 10 per cent for the World Class Tests is analogous to that of the 10 per cent cut-off by Intelligence Quotient of 119 in an intelligence test. The distribution of IQ is assumed to be normal and is encapsulated in the disarmingly simple looking formula:

$$IQ \sim N(100,15)$$

So the 119 score is slightly above one standard deviation beyond the population mean of 100.

The assumption that problem solving ability and mathematical ability are normally distributed over the world population makes it conceptually possible to think in terms of the top 10 per cent. Knowledge of the mean and standard deviation – or even the probability density function – for the World Class Tests is not a requirement for parents and teachers likely to steer children towards taking the tests. However, the purpose of the tests is fundamentally different from intelligence testing, which could result in scores well to the left of the mean. Since a score of one standard deviation above the mean is sufficient to cut off 10 per cent, it is hoped that children taking the tests will somehow be judged, accurately, to be in the region of a standard deviation above the mean.

From a practical point of view, the extent to which the density functions for problem solving ability and mathematical ability coincide is of interest to parents and teachers because of the implications for training and assessment – both before and after taking the tests.

Shuffling the results

At this juncture, a 'thought experiment' may be productive:

- First, imagine a geographical region split into educational units. The region may be a country or a local authority district; the educational units may be local authority districts or schools.
- Assume that each educational unit has sought to find, using the World Class Tests, its top 10 per cent in problem solving and mathematics. The 10 per cent would relate to the total number of students in the educational unit.
- Then assume that the results from all the educational units were shuffled together; the resulting set would consist of the top 10 per cent of the region and would relate to the total number of students in the region.
- Now imagine what would happen if, instead of shuffling the results, each educational unit ranked its results in descending order of scores. Suppose that a sorting algorithm were employed to merge the ranked scores of the units to obtain a ranked list – for each test – for the whole region. It is likely that extra scores would need to be brought in from the higher performing units and some scores from the lower units deleted – with each additional score one deletion would be required. In this way, a ranked 10 per cent for each test for the whole region would be obtained.

The results of such a merging and sorting algorithm being used on the test scores are likely to produce:

- an uneven distribution of the top 10 per cent of the region over the educational units;
- a membership of the 10 per cent problem solving category not coinciding with the 10 per cent mathematics category.

These snapshots of the distribution of the top 10 per cent of performers in each test could provide the basis of intervention and support strategies for national education policy makers.

SUBMERGED TALENT

Reflection on the above thought experiment leads to an important practical consideration, which is presented in the form of a basic diagram (see Figure 8.1).

Let a rectangle represent the total population of students of a region. One rectangle could be used to represent the region's nine year olds, another could represent its 13 year olds. The following argument applies to each age group equally.

Figure 8.1: *The nine year old population*

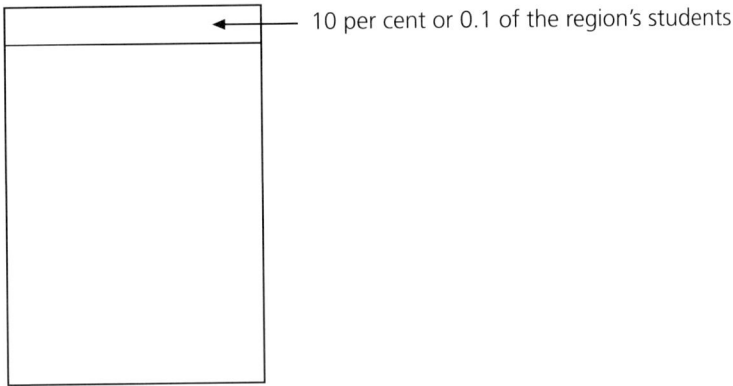

10 per cent or 0.1 of the region's students

Our experience and teachers' comments suggest that, when the tests are tried in two educational units of widely differing social and economic attributes, access to the tests may not be available to all students. The reality of such a testing situation is more likely to be represented by the following diagram (Figure 8.2), with X per cent of the children being excluded from consideration.

Figure 8.2: *The reduced nine year old population*

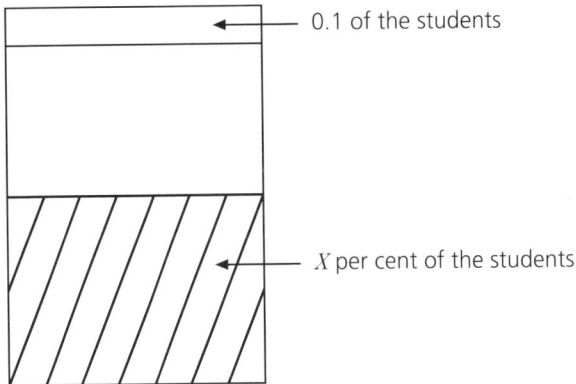

0.1 of the students

X per cent of the students

It is conjectured that the X per cent will be greater in areas of relative deprivation and less in areas of relative affluence, and that some of the top 10 per cent may form part of that X per cent. Hence the 0.1 of students found to form the set of world class performers will be 0.1 of $(1-X)$, not 0.1 of 1.

In reality, the lines at the top of the rectangle representing X require gaps to correspond to the degree of social closure; the smaller the gaps the greater the social closure within the regions. Social closure, a phenomenon studied by Murphy (1988) refers to the process of subordination, 'whereby one group monopolises advantage by closing off opportunities to another group that it defines as inferior and ineligible'. The reality of the phenomenon in the UK has been investigated by the Institute for Fiscal Studies (Johnson and Reed, 1996). A conclusion of *Two Nations? The Inheritance of Poverty and Affluence* is that 'able children of poor parents do have a better chance of moving into higher income bands that do the less able children'. It is hoped that the implementation of *Excellence in Cities* will not only provide an increased income, but that it will also initiate a move from State 1 to State 2, as shown in Figure 8.3, showing wider gaps above the X rectangle for State 2.

Figure 8.3: *Increasing social inclusion*

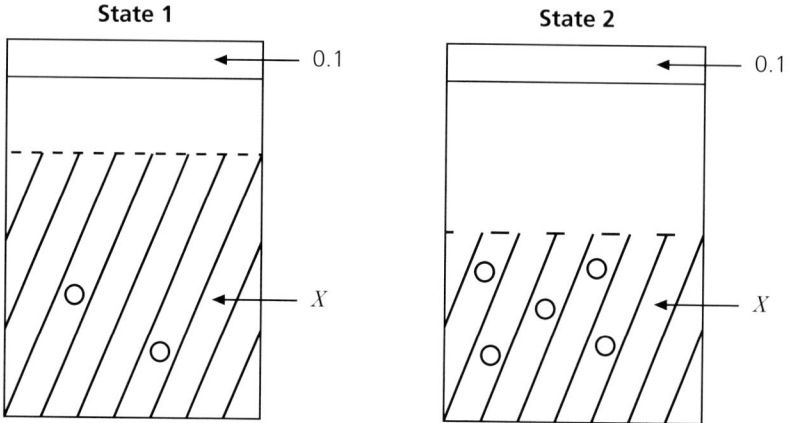

A decrease in X from State 1 to State 2 at some time in the future will require a reduction in the amount of submerged talent, the value of X and a decrease in the forces of social closure, the gaps at the top of the X section. This will be equivalent to bubbles of talent being detected and allowed to rise to form part of the 10 per cent of world-class performers.

Pertinent questions relating to the existence of 'talent bubbles' are:
• How do deprivation indicators point towards the destruction of talent bubbles, preventing them from floating into the top 10 per cent and consequently becoming unfulfilled lives, in some cases becoming diverted towards violence and crime?
• What policy parameters can contribute to the reduction of social closure and so enhance social justice?

Case study

FIELDWORK AND METHODS

The data used for this chapter, based on a single case study, was collected for the purpose of highlighting the viability of using the World Class Tests as a means of searching for talents in inner-city areas where there is a high level of deprivation and underachievement. An 'opportunity sample' (Brown and Dowling, 1999) for the case study was provided within the context of the work of the BACE centre, which offers professional development courses for teachers and extension programmes for gifted and talented children. The data reported in this study was drawn from a project commissioned by an LEA 'Action Zone' in 1999, completing in 2001. An Action Zone is a group of schools committed to raising standards in their area; for further details please see Appendix 1, page 127.

The project consisted of two strands: a professional development programme for teachers and an extension programme for identified high ability students from their schools. The sample studied consisted of 15 primary school teachers and 20 nine year old children, hitherto referred to as the case study teachers and students. The students were selected from schools of the Education Action Zone on the basis of their potential ability rather than their performance in written tests. It should be noted that some of the schools in the Action Zone are on 'special measures' for improvement in achievement as a result of inspections by the Office for Standards in Education (OfSTED). The LEA where the schools are located is also amongst the lowest 10 of over 140 LEAs in the League Tables for their performance in the national tests. It is against this background that the Action Zone decided to commission a project in order to encourage their schools to search for and fulfil potential talent. As teachers felt that the identification of gifted and talented students in schools where a high proportion of students achieved low test-results was particularly difficult, the BACE centre issued them with a checklist, based on observation of behaviours, to select students for the extension programme. Just by coincidence these students were taught at the University by an associate lecturer, Eileen, who worked in the highest achieving school in a Local Education Authority which is amongst the top four in the national League Tables for achievement.

The first spark of interest for this pilot study was provided by comments made by Eileen during one of her conversations with the authors very early in the teaching programme. The summary of her comments was that although in their knowledge of facts and skills the case study students showed many gaps, in problem solving situations many of them were as good as, or sometimes better than, the children in her own school. As the authors and Eileen could only speculate on the reasons for this observation, it was decided to conduct a study that might provide some evidence to substantiate Eileen's observations. At the time of teaching the case study students on the extension programme, Eileen had been invited by QCA to trial some of the World Class Tests materials in mathematics and problem-solving. As she was familiar with the tests, it was decided that Eileen would use the published exemplar World Class Tests materials as part of the case study. The authors were interested in two types of data: teachers' perceptions of the role of the World Class Tests for their students and the observations of students' responses to problem-solving activities, which included items from the World Class Tests. Data for both types were collected over a period of two months through the following means:

- the authors' open-ended interviews with Eileen delivering the extension programme;
- the authors' notes on discussions with teachers on their perceptions of the role of the World Class Tests in their schools;
- observation of students working with mathematics and problem solving material which also included the World Class Tests;
- comparison of test results of a group of case-study students with that of a group of nine year olds from a high attaining school in a high attaining LEA.

The fieldwork focused on one case study, a single instance or one unit of analysis. This choice is justified because of its intrinsic interest (Gall *et al.*, 1996) and the unique opportunity provided by this case to shed light on aspects of a radical new initiative introduced by the British government. The findings are, however, tentative and only a first attempt to conceptualise ideas within the framework of the identification and

111

fulfilment of talent. Further, only pencil and paper test items were used to assess students' performance in the World Class Tests. This adds to the limitations of any claims made. It is accepted that the findings of this small study can only be generalised if they are applicable to other situations. However, the results may serve the purpose of a documentary in highlighting issues of interest.

FINDINGS

The findings of this pilot study need to be considered bearing in mind the limitations of using a small sample. Some significant issues that arose from the study are presented here with evidence collected from the four sets of data mentioned in the previous section. Only snapshots are provided.

Eileen's comments

Eileen's initial comment was that the case study students' problem-solving skills were either 'as good as' or, in some cases 'better' than, that that of the children in her school. On probing she explained these skills as 'swiftness of response' and 'reasoning skills'. However, Eileen observed that when children needed to apply mathematical skills to problem-solving activities, they were often 'stuck'.

Students' responses to problem solving

In order to investigate Eileen's comments from the previous section further, a group of four students were given a problem solving activity, 'Rabbits and Hutches' (Burton, 1986):

> *There are some rabbits and some rabbit hutches. If seven rabbits are put in each hutch, one rabbit is left over. If nine rabbits are put in each rabbit hutch, one hutch is left empty. Can you find how many rabbit hutches and how many rabbits there are?*

Three out of the four students were able to explain what the problem meant and draw diagrams to represent the ideas, but were unable to select and perform the necessary calculations in order to solve the problem. After a short teaching session on how to work out bonds of sevens and nines, all three arrived at an answer quickly. One of the students also produced an explanation of how she figured it out.

Teachers' perceptions of the role and use of World Class Tests

As part of the professional development programme, a session was devoted to introducing participating teachers to the World Class Tests initiative. Their comments and observations were recorded. The following initial comments, before they were given the exemplar test items and students' responses to the test items, were of interest to the researchers:

> *It is unlikely that any of our children will get anywhere near them. There will be a stampede of middle class and independent school parents wanting to enter their kids.*
> *Our children will never have the ability to take these tests. We don't have any really gifted children in our school.*
> *Teachers don't know how to teach problem solving. It is not part of the national curriculum.*
> *With the kind of social and discipline problems we have, and the supply teacher shortages, we won't have the time to even tell the parents about these tests.*

These perceptions were somewhat changed after the teachers were given opportunities to review the World Class Tests material on the web. They were also shown how the children in their schools responded to the test items verbally and on paper. Amongst the positive comments that emerged as a result of this were some about the 'high quality of the content' and about how the activities were motivating. They felt that the problem solving materials could serve as a 'means of identification'. The importance of making the test available within the schools, especially in their local area, was also emphasised.

The two groups of children and their performance

The two groups involved in trialling the World Class Tests, in problem solving and mathematics, had both been taught by Eileen, a very effective Year 4 teacher, within the geographical area providing Group A. Group B, from the deprived area, had also been taught by her for about half a year on Saturdays. The tests used were for nine year old children and were downloaded from the internet.

Eileen selected for participation in the trialling, based on her experience and observation, the top five children in each of the classes to form Group A and Group B.

Marking

In order to maximise uniformity of treatment, devising the marking scheme and marking of the tests were made the responsibility of one person. Ten marks were allocated to each question, with a portion of the marks being awarded to indications of working when such indications were judged to be appropriate.

Test results

The results in the two tests for each group of five children are shown in Tables 8.1 to 8.4 (below). Child B4, in Group B, was withdrawn from the mathematics test because Eileen observed the child becoming tearful.

Table 8.1: *Problem Solving – Group A (Affluent)*

	Q1	Q2	Q3	Q4	Q5	Q6	TOTAL	TOP 5 RANKING MAX = 60
A1	6	0	0	6	6	0	18	–
A2	6	2	0	6	10	0	24	5
A3	6	6	2	6	0	0	20	–
A4	6	0	0	8	8	0	22	–
A5	3	10	2	8	8	0	31	3

Table 8.2: *Problem Solving – Group B (Deprived)*

	Q1	Q2	Q3	Q4	Q5	Q6	TOTAL	TOP 5 RANKING MAX = 60
B1	6	10	2	6	6	10	40	1
B2	6	10	2	4	4	10	36	2
B3	6	5	0	6	10	0	27	4
B4	6	0	0	8	4	0	18	–
B5	6	5	0	0	2	3	16	–

Table 8.3: *Mathematics – Group A (Affluent)*

	Q1	Q2	Q3	Q4	Q5	Q6	Q7	TOTAL	TOP 5 RANKING MAX = 70
A1	0	10	10	10	10	3	0	43	3
A2	0	0	0	0	10	3	6	19	–
A3	7	0	0	0	0	10	2	19	–
A4	0	6	10	10	0	10	10	46	2
A5	0	0	10	0	10	7	3	30	4

Table 8.4: *Mathematics – Group B (Deprived)*

	Q1	Q2	Q3	Q4	Q5	Q6	Q7	TOTAL	TOP 5 RANKING MAX = 70
B1	10	10	10	10	10	7	10	67	1
B2	0	0	10	10	10	0	0	30	4
B3	0	0	0	0	0	0	0	0	–
B4	Withdrawn from test								
B5	0	0	0	10	0	0	0	10	–

Comments

When the marks for the problem solving test were merged and ranked, three of the top five positions were taken by Group B children.

When the marks for the mathematics test were merged and rounded, three of the top five positions were taken by Group A children.

Such a small sample can, of course, only suggest conjectures for further investigation, but it seems that Group B children were more adept at problem solving than Group A children who, in turn, were better at mathematics. Group A children seemed better equipped with basic knowledge and skills; questions on decimals and negative numbers – particularly for Group B – fell on an epistemological wasteland.

A tentative model for the children involved could be represented diagrammatically thinking of the child as an information processor, as in Figure 8.4 (opposite).

Perhaps Group B's performance in problem solving was due to greater competence with visual or diagrammatic images (V) and the relatively poor performance in mathematics due to lesser exposure to high-quality natural language (N), less training in manipulating symbolic or numbers and operations (S) and greater susceptibility of bubbles of talent to burst due to deprivation (D).

It is possible to take the small sample on suggesting submerged talent having been discovered in the area of relative deprivation.

The national and international education policy implication may be that problem solving, if found within the submerged talent of a deprived area, could contribute to future technological innovation. This suggestion relates to the concept of endogenous economic growth, based on Josef Schumpeter's notion (Schumpeter, 1969) of creative destruction. As Aghion and Howitt (1998) indicate:

> The purpose of endogenous growth theory is to reach some understanding of the interplay between technological knowledge and various structural characterisation of the economy, and society, and how such an interplay results in economic growth.

The possibility of forms of social closure and deprivation being amongst those structural characteristics seems worthy of investigation. Bubbles of talent, submerged, could contribute to growth if allowed to float into the top 10 per cent.

Figure 8.4: *An information-processing child*

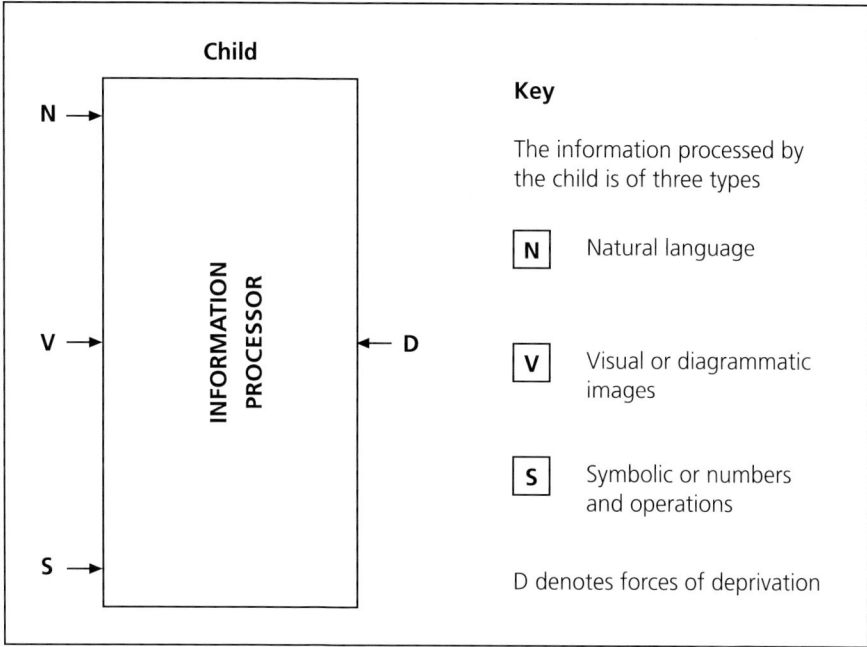

Some professional development issues for consideration

The following observations are made on the basis of studying aspects of using the World Class Tests within the present study, the test results and the interaction with teachers who participated in the professional development programmes offered by the BACE centre.

- There seems to be a misconception amongst some teachers that it is unlikely to find gifted and talented children in schools where there is low achievement in national tests and a high level of problems due to social deprivation. On the basis of the evidence gathered during the project the researchers feel that the World Class Tests in problem solving may in fact provide a means of identifying and recognising talent within these situations. Replication of the pilot study with a larger sample of schools and children may provide support for using the problem solving tests as a means of identification of high ability in areas within the *Excellence in Cities* programme.
- The World Class Tests offered by the UK government should be adopted as a means of identification and recognition of talent. Proposed new developments such as a national centre for gifted and talented students should use the World Class Tests for selection of students for special programmes.
- A professional development programme which provides information on the World Class Tests, its rationale, its design and hands-on experience of the tests would be worthwhile. Such programmes could draw on students' responses to test items. Such a programme would enhance teachers' abilities to make effective identification of talent and to adopt sound teaching strategies for their able students.

- The evidence from the present study suggests that high ability students may not necessarily perform in mathematics at a level consistent with their ability if their knowledge of mathematical facts and skills are low. This may lead to the non-identification of gifted students.
- Three questions frequently asked by teachers are, 'Can problem-solving attributes provide an indicator of high ability?' ' Can children be trained in problem solving?' and 'Does developing problem-solving ability enhance general achievement?' None of these questions has hitherto been targeted for research in England and Wales. The experience of the authors suggests that all are worthy of it.
- It would be useful to monitor the numbers of students taking the World Class Tests from areas of social deprivation and take appropriate action if the take-up in these areas is low.

Concluding remarks

A sample of World Class Tests has produced data of performance in the problem solving and mathematics tests for nine year olds, of groups of children from two very different socio-economic backgrounds. If such testing was replicated more extensively in the two educational units and over the whole region a benchmark of performance, the World Class Tests, could give a distribution of talent over the whole region. If the same were done with the test for 13 year olds, then the tests could be considered to provide a two-stage benchmark for identifying the distribution of talent in problem solving and mathematics.

Since the UK is a G7 country, the tests may be considered to have suggested the existence of submerged talent within an advanced industrialised country requiring action, in support of *Excellence in Cities*, to reduce social closure and contribute to future economic growth – of the endogenous as well as the exogenous kind. Tentative inferences may be drawn about how education policies may be monitored, using the World Class Tests, to gauge possibilities for decreasing social closure, releasing submerged talent and enhancing future growth.

The World Bank uses the acronym ECD to refer to Early Childhood Development and UNICEF (2001) defines ECD as a 'comprehensive approach to policies and programmes for children from birth to eight years of age, their parents and caregivers. Its purpose is to protect the child's rights to develop his or her full cognitive, emotional, social and physical potential'.

Excellence in Cities may be regarded as part of an extension of the ECD approach to children within a G7 country. Could the extensive use of World Class Tests provide the educational levels to enhance lifelong possibilities for a broad range of children – even beyond the 10 per cent and within the X per cent residing within deprived areas?

Perhaps the broad ranging objectives specified by UNICEF of ECD would, with appropriate supplementary policies on child poverty, lead to an enhanced and more enlightened world with the release of submerged talent.

One more Mandela; one less Ossama bin Laden. An increase in bubbles of talent rising; a decrease in bombs of terrorism. Why not let idealism be skewed towards hope, and World Class Tests be assumed symmetrically normal? Then, perhaps, as more and more submerged talent receives the acclaim of world-class recognition, more and more children will, in the words of Kofi Annan, 'contribute to society in meaningful ways'.

9 Screening for academic talent through above-level assessment: the Australian Primary Talent Search

Rosalind Elder
Gifted Education Research, Resource and Information Centre (GERRIC)
University of New South Wales, Sydney, Australia

Introduction

GERRIC

GERRIC – THE GIFTED EDUCATION RESEARCH, RESOURCE AND INFORMATION CENTRE – is a self-funding centre in the School of Education at the University of New South Wales. The Centre was established in 1997, although many of its courses and activities had been operating informally for 10 years prior to this. The Centre is committed to meeting the educational, social and emotional needs of gifted children and adolescents by conducting and fostering research and by providing services to these children, their families and schools.

In 1998 GERRIC embarked on a venture in partnership with its sister centre – the Belin-Blank International Center for Gifted Education and Talent Development at the University of Iowa, USA – to extend its talent search programme to Australia.

THE AUSTRALIAN PRIMARY TALENT SEARCH

A critical issue in identifying academically gifted students is the problem of ceiling effect, which may affect the accuracy of assessment when these students are assessed on a test designed for age-peers. Age-appropriate tests do not often possess enough discriminatory power to accurately assess the aptitude or achievements of high ability learners.

Australia, unlike the United States, has no tradition of standardised testing in primary school, which has required the development of other selection criteria – including the use of IQ or achievement test results, results on state-wide or national

For brief notes on the Australian education system, please see page 129.

competitions, placement in school gifted programmes, or teacher nomination.

Since 1998, more than 3,800 academically gifted students in Grades 3 to 6 have participated in the Australian Primary Talent Search (APTS), a programme conducted by GERRIC in conjunction with the Belin-Blank Center. Students applying to take *EXPLORE*, an above-level test normed on Grade 8 students in America, are required to provide evidence of high academic potential to participate in the testing programme.

This chapter will examine results from the APTS testing and discuss the implications of these results for the effectiveness of different methods of identifying academically gifted students.

The Talent Search Model

The talent search model was pioneered in the USA during the 1930s by psychologist Leta Stetter Hollingworth and later by Dr Julian Stanley of Johns Hopkins University. The model seeks to identify exceptional talent through the use of above-level testing. Above-level testing is an educational technique whereby tests designed for older students are administered to younger students who have already reached the ceiling on tests designed for their age or grade level.

Hansen (1992) describes the ceiling effect as 'the clustering of scores at the upper limit of the test'. She goes on to explain (p.11) that while high scores may please educators, in reality they may provide very little diagnostic information about the person being tested:

> For the highly gifted child, grade level test scores tell only the percentage of students that performs below the individual but obscure what the child could have achieved had the test included appropriately difficult items.

On-grade assessments do not allow us to differentiate among high scoring children those who may have simply mastered the material that is being tested, and those who have the ability to go far in advance of it. Above-level testing allows us to note distinctions between high ability students whose educational needs may be very different.

Olszewski-Kubilius (1994) argues that the talent search model is beneficial because it:

- **is cost effective and efficient** – a large number of students can be tested relatively cheaply, giving parents a comprehensive assessment of their child's need for acceleration, curriculum compacting, early entrance into tertiary study, and so on.
- **is based on sound educational principles and practices** – above-level testing serves to differentiate between those students who are at the ceiling of on-level tests.
- **is consistent with students' development** – students' abilities become more specialised as they enter high school, therefore tests that concentrate on specific domains of ability, rather than overall general ability, are better indicators of specific academic aptitude.
- **guides educational planning** – by differentiating between the moderately and highly gifted, talent searches can provide invaluable knowledge for educators about the types of educational programmes needed to develop students' potential to its fullest.

- **promotes programmes** – Olszewski-Kubilius directly attributes the growth of educational programmes and opportunities for gifted students to the talent search model.

Talent searches also provide the administrative centre with a database on the characteristics, educational needs and learning styles of the students who are identified. It is now standard practice for GERRIC, for example, to include with Talent Search enrolment materials, questionnaires for both parents and students: these include items that investigate attributions of success and failure, parental involvement in the student's school, and home life. GERRIC and the Belin-Blank Centre are engaged in ongoing cross-cultural research using data collected in this way.

EXPLORE

Students in Grades 3 to 6 who register with GERRIC for the Australian Primary Talent Search (APTS) take a test called *EXPLORE*, developed by American College Testing (ACT, 1995). *EXPLORE* is normed on eighth grade students and is used to assess readiness to enter high school in the USA. It is a multiple choice test, which assesses four areas of student ability:

- **English** consists of 40 items and is divided into two sub-tests: usage/mechanics and rhetorical skills. The usage/mechanics sub-test examines students' understanding of standard written English. The rhetorical skills sub-test measures students' grasp of strategy, organisation, and style in writing.
- **Mathematics** has 30 items, which measure mathematical reasoning rather than simply the ability to memorise formulas or carry out involved calculations. Test items cover three areas – basic skills, application, and analysis – in pre-algebra, elementary algebra, geometry, statistics and probability.
- **Reading** comprises 30 items that measure reading comprehension by focusing on the skills needed when studying written materials from different subject areas.
- **Science reasoning** consists of 20 items that measure scientific reasoning skills. There are six sets of scientific information in one of three different formats: data representation, research summaries and conflicting viewpoints. The test measures how well students understand scientific information and draw conclusions.

Each test lasts 30 minutes and test scores are scaled to marks between 1 and 25. All students who register for the test sit for all four tests, regardless of where their area of talent lies. GERRIC has found that high ability students may underestimate their abilities in areas they believe to be a relative 'weakness'.

SELECTION OF STUDENTS

Traditionally the talent search model has used the results of standardised tests to screen students for participation in the talent search. The feasibility of running APTS in Australia was initially hampered by the size of the country and the spread of population. Given that the talent search model requires pre-selection of those students who have already performed at the 95th percentile or above on a standardised test, only the top 5 per cent of a single grade are eligible to be tested. Identifying students who were testing already at the 95th percentile was difficult because of the general lack of standardised testing in Australian primary schools.

This dearth of standardised testing in Australian schools has meant that GERRIC has had to develop procedures by which to identify students who would be suitable candidates. We needed to find methods of identification which would not require schools to invest enormous amounts of time, personnel and money: after all, the aim of the talent search was to assist schools, as efficiently and effectively as possible, rather than to create more work.

As Australia's *de facto* national centre for gifted education, GERRIC realised that any set of selection criteria that it employed and published would swiftly be adopted by schools and other organisations as entrance criteria for other programmes around the country.

In consultation with educators from other states, GERRIC compiled a list of qualifying criteria. A student would be eligible for testing if he or she had evidence of any of the following:

- a score at or above the 95th percentile (indicating an IQ of 125+) on any individual or group IQ test or a subscale (for example, verbal or performance subscales) of an individual IQ test. We included IQ subscale scores to ensure that we were not excluding students who were gifted but suffered from a learning disability.
- a score at or above the 95th percentile on a standardised test of achievement in any academic subject area. There were very few students who used this as a criterion for entry, however, some of the tests cited included: the *Neale Analysis of Reading Ability* (Neale, 1999), the *Tests of Reading Comprehension (TORCH)* (ACER,1987) and the *Progressive Achievement Tests (PAT)* (ACER, 1985, 1987).
- a score well within the top band of any of the state-wide basic skills tests. There is some testing of basic competencies in Queensland, Victoria and New South Wales, but traditionally these are multiple choice tests, with very low ceilings and virtually no power of discrimination for gifted students.
- a placement in a full-time, self-contained class for academically gifted students. Over 100 such classes exist in New South Wales and a few in other states too.
- an award of an academic scholarship.
- a Distinction or High Distinction in the Australian Schools Science or English competitions, or the Australian Primary Mathematics Competition. These are off-level tests that do not require curriculum specific knowledge; they are offered by the University of New South Wales as competitions from Grade 3 upwards and are similar to tests of aptitude and reasoning skills.
- a letter of support from his or her teacher, who believes that he or she has the academic potential to perform at a level well above the expected grade level in an academic area.

The purpose of these criteria was not to render the test exclusive, but rather to give parents and teachers guidelines for identifying those students who might most benefit from testing. Without sufficiently broad criteria, we could simply have been confirming societal and teacher prejudices, which may have hindered equitable access to the test. Additionally, we were able to provide access via the internet to practice questions that allowed students, parents and teachers to determine whether a student might be unduly frustrated by the content of the tests. The criteria were established to ensure that the children who took the test would not experience anxiety or be faced with material far beyond their capabilities.

Schools were approached at the beginning of the Australian school year (January) to act as test centres. Once the test sites had been established across the country, schools were sent information packs to distribute to eligible students. Parents were responsible for registering their children for testing. To ensure that no child was denied access to the test through financial constraints, parents who were recipients of government social security benefits were exempted from the testing fee.

Parental involvement allowed the enrolment in the testing programme of children attending schools that did not conduct standardised testing. The results of *EXPLORE* are sent to the parents of students, and to the schools, if requested by the parents. The APTS Interpretation Guide encourages parents to share the results of the testing with teachers, and gives strategies by which both parents and teachers can interpret and apply the results.

RESULTS OF TESTING

Prior to the initial testing in 1998, five Sydney schools piloted the Australian Primary Talent Search with small numbers of students. In 1998, GERRIC tested 1,085 students in New South Wales and the Australian Capital Territory (ACT). In 1999 the test was offered Australia-wide and over 1,800 students were tested. In 2000, 1,400 students took the test. In 2001 a further 1,500 students registered for testing.

The results have provided a disturbing indictment of the level of the work presented in the regular primary school classroom, as more than 50 per cent of the Grade 4, 5 and 6 testers have scored above the mean of the Grade 8 norms in one or more of the tests. Table 9.1 (see below) shows the mean scores for Australian students from 1998 to 2000. The average scores for US eighth graders are shown in the bottom row of the table by way of comparison. Gifted Australian fifth grade students gained scores above the scores of average Grade 8 students in *every* area except mathematics.

Table 9.1: *Australian and US means (1998–2000) by school grade and subject*

GRADE	ENGLISH	MATHS	READING	SCIENCE	COMPOSITE	n
Grade 3	11.1	9.9	9.4	11.6	10.6	102
Grade 4	12.9	11.1	11.3	13.6	12.4	1,132
Grade 5	15.3	13.6	14.3	15.8	14.9	1,306
Grade 6	17.3	16.1	17.0	17.8	17.2	1,364
US Grade 8	14.0	14.3	13.6	14.1	14.1	

Even though a few students in Grades 4 to 6 attain the maximum scale score of 25, research by ACT has demonstrated that, in general, the EXPLORE tests have enough difficult items to challenge APTS participants, and to avoid the ceiling effect operating. These general results also suggest that the APTS participants are not unnecessarily frustrated by the more challenging questions.

(GERRIC 2000, p.14).

PRACTICAL APPLICATION

The primary goal of APTS is to provide parents and schools with information about the gifted student that can be translated into appropriate differentiated curricula within the school. Included with the *EXPLORE* results is a document entitled *The Standards for Transition* (ACT, 1997). This document allows parents and teachers to align a student's scores with curriculum outcomes, to use this diagnostic information to locate the student in the sequence of core curriculum outcomes and engage in planning a suitable curriculum for the student.

The pyramid of curricular options for Talent Search participants (Figure 9.1) shows 13 educational options recommended for talent search participants, ranging from the least accelerative to the most accelerative. From this array of options educators may select the most appropriate combination of interventions for the student.

Figure 9.1: *Pyramid of curricular options for Talent Search participants*

This figure was adapted with permission from a book chapter by Susan Assouline and Ann Lupkowski-Shoplik, which appears in the second edition of Handbook of Gifted Education, by Nicholas Colangelo and Gary Davis, published by Allyn and Bacon, Needham Heights, MA USA in 1997.

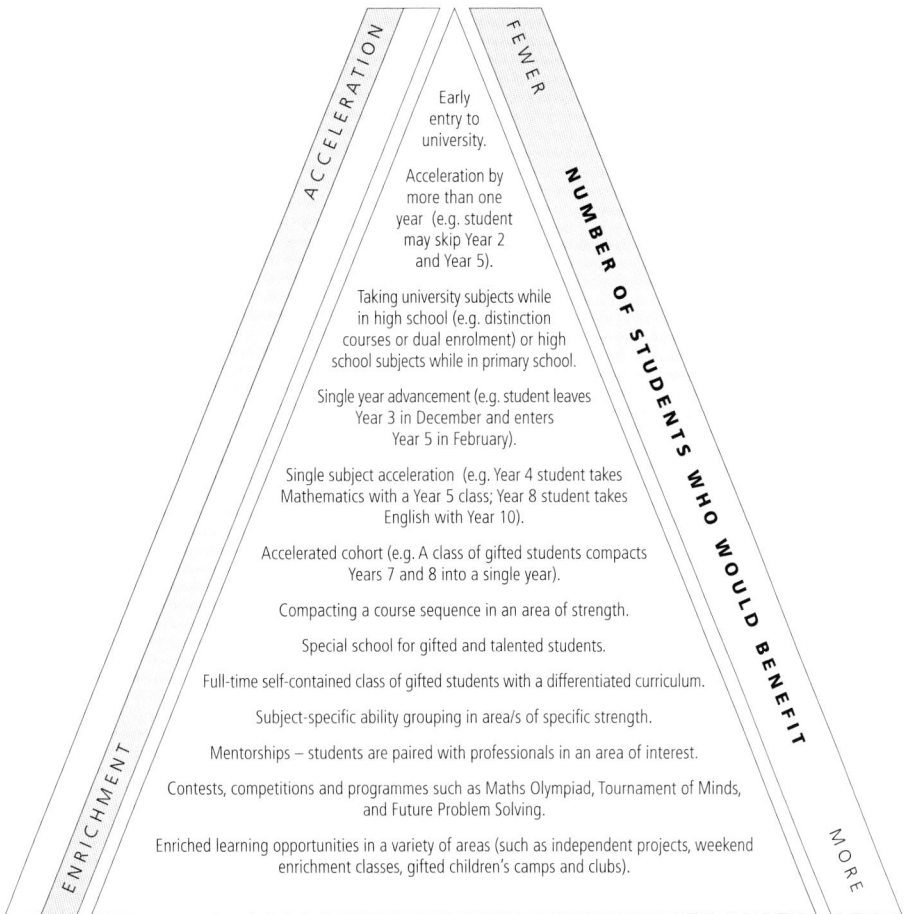

ACCELERATION — FEWER — NUMBER OF STUDENTS WHO WOULD BENEFIT

Early entry to university.

Acceleration by more than one year (e.g. student may skip Year 2 and Year 5).

Taking university subjects while in high school (e.g. distinction courses or dual enrolment) or high school subjects while in primary school.

Single year advancement (e.g. student leaves Year 3 in December and enters Year 5 in February).

Single subject acceleration (e.g. Year 4 student takes Mathematics with a Year 5 class; Year 8 student takes English with Year 10).

Accelerated cohort (e.g. A class of gifted students compacts Years 7 and 8 into a single year).

Compacting a course sequence in an area of strength.

Special school for gifted and talented students.

Full-time self-contained class of gifted students with a differentiated curriculum.

Subject-specific ability grouping in area/s of specific strength.

Mentorships – students are paired with professionals in an area of interest.

Contests, competitions and programmes such as Maths Olympiad, Tournament of Minds, and Future Problem Solving.

Enriched learning opportunities in a variety of areas (such as independent projects, weekend enrichment classes, gifted children's camps and clubs).

ENRICHMENT — MORE

The accelerative options include a wide variety of strategies designed to allow the student to move through the curriculum at a pace that is commensurate with their ability.

The most accelerative options in the pyramid are recommended for those students who scored above the 50th percentile, as compared to US eighth grade students, in a particular subject area on *EXPLORE*. This pyramid of options is included with the *EXPLORE* results, which parents of APTS students are encouraged to discuss with their teacher or co-ordinator of gifted students.

Some schools have been marvellously responsive to the process, as one teacher writes:
There are students in our college whose lives have been changed due to the evidence of their abilities uncovered by EXPLORE. This evidence could not be found to the same degree or detail with PAT testing, NSW Competitions, basic skills testing, class testing or diagnostic school ability testing. In its form and reporting, APTS is a standout.

The solid evidence of scientific, mathematical and English reasoning ability shown on a single A4 piece of paper has been instrumental in identifying the need for adequate educational challenge for a number of students in the college. EXPLORE results achieved two years before were the most valuable piece of evidence when investigating the boredom and frustration of a high achieving Year 8 student. These results differentiated her from gifted peers where traditional forms of testing couldn't. The implications of the results were readily understood by her high school teachers and assisted me in advocating for grade acceleration as an option to meet her educational needs. With a Year 6 EXPLORE science reasoning ability close to the 100th percentile, it is not surprising that this Year 10 student has been accelerated again in science and is embracing her studies with commitment and passion.

The science component of the test has also been marvellous in the early identification of science reasoning ability and has been partly instrumental in a science program being developed in our…college whereby high school science staff instruct students in Years 5 and 6.

(Mackie, 2001)

Outcomes

SUCCESS OF THE QUALIFYING CRITERIA

The results gained by Australian students demonstrated that qualifying criteria for APTS developed by GERRIC were successful in providing a guide to parents and teachers as to which students would be the most appropriate candidates for above-level assessment.

Table 9.2 (page 124) shows the mean composite scores (a combination of the English, mathematics, reading and science reasoning test scale scores) for each of the qualifying criteria for Grade 5 and 6 students. (Note: only Grades 5 and 6 have been included as some qualifying information was not applicable to Grades 3 and 4. For example, entry into a self-contained gifted class typically begins at Grade 5). This table should be interpreted with caution. It is not possible to draw conclusions about the most successful predictor of success on the talent search instrument as many children met more than one criterion to sit the test. However it is interesting to note the differences in the mean scores between the methods of qualification, especially with regard to those students who were nominated by teachers. Research conducted over the years (Jacobs, 1971; Hall, 1983; Pegnato and Birch, 1957) has confirmed that untrained teachers are poor identifiers of gifted children. With most undergraduate teachers in Australia receiving no more than one hour's pre-service training in gifted education it is surprising that teachers did so well in nominating gifted students. Of course, we have no indication of whether the teachers nominating students for APTS were trained or untrained in gifted education, but they must have had at least a passing interest in the needs of gifted children to have nominated students to become involved in the programme.

On the whole, students who qualified for APTS on the basis of teacher nomination did not fulfil any of the other criteria. While the difference in mean scores is statistically significant, it is hard to argue the practical significance of two scaled marks.

Table 9.2: *Means for students in Grades 5 and 6 in 1998–99, by method of qualifying*

METHOD FOR QUALIFYING FOR APTS	MEAN	SD	n
IQ test full scale 125+	16.10	3.38	183
Subscale 125+	14.95	3.44	37
95th percentile on standardised achievement test	15.11	3.11	61
Top band of basic skills	15.42	3.02	269
Self-contained class for gifted students	16.92	2.78	183
Distinction or High Distinction in University of New South Wales competition	16.66	3.26	703
Teacher nomination	14.10	3.14	248

GERRIC PROGRAMMES FOR APTS STUDENTS

The primary goal of the Australian Primary Talent Search is to assist parents and teachers in educational planning for gifted students. At the grassroots level this depends on the responsiveness of teachers and schools to the educational needs of these students. On-going teacher in-service training conducted by GERRIC for education systems and groups of schools across Australia has meant that more teachers are becoming aware of these special needs.

All students who participate in the Australian Primary Talent Search are eligible to participate in GERRIC's holiday enrichment programmes for gifted students. These programmes are offered twice a year, in the summer and winter vacations, and attract more than 1,000 students on each occasion to the University of New South Wales. Additionally GERRIC has developed residential programmes for high scoring students, with the aim of fostering their talents and providing them with an opportunity to mix with other students of similar ability.

Since January 1999 GERRIC has offered between 60 and 70 places in a week-long residential camp for students who have obtained extremely high scores in APTS. These programmes give gifted students a week of intensive, fast-paced, high level study in their talent area, and also provide a week of interaction with like-minded students. In fact, the affective aspects of the week have probably been the more important feature for the majority of students attending.

The academic workshops are conducted by teachers who not only have postgraduate qualifications in gifted education, but who also have considerable experience of teaching academically gifted students. The workshop content is academically rigorous and fast-paced, with these primary students typically working on material not usually presented until the final years of high school.

Students are not formally evaluated on their performance in the workshops. Instead each workshop gives a presentation to an audience of parents, siblings and other workshop participants, allowing students to demonstrate the learning that has taken place over the week to an interested audience in an intellectually and emotionally safe environment.

LESSONS TO BE LEARNED

Non-standardised methods of identifying candidates for above-level testing can be highly effective. Traditionally the talent searches of the United States have relied primarily on students' test scores to identify them for above-level testing. GERRIC's trials of competition results, academic scholarships and teacher nomination have shown that these methods are also worthy of consideration. In a country such as Australia, which has a traditional wariness of large-scale standardised testing, informal and flexible methods of identification are both necessary and effective.

A heavy reliance on teacher nomination may not necessarily yield the best candidates, unless the nominating teachers have had training in identifying gifted children. We know that gifted children's talents will not necessarily be recognised where whole class teaching is used and in classrooms where the expectations for all students are based on chronological age rather than individual ability, as the gifted students may not have the opportunity to display their abilities.

The Talent Search should be designed to be inclusive. If children are eager to participate, they should be permitted to. The screening process is designed to ensure that no child is made to feel anxious by being asked to sit a test that is too difficult – it is not about eliminating students who could benefit. As children get older they become more a realistic source of self-nomination (Gross, 1999). GERRIC uses self-nomination as the primary criterion for extra-curricular accelerative enrichment high school programmes. GERRIC has found that, given ample information about the content and demands of a programme, most teenagers can make an informed and accurate assessment of the suitability of the programme in matching their needs. Obviously there are cases of over- and under-estimation by both parents and teachers, and circumstances in which children from differing backgrounds, experience and exposure need encouragement to engage with educational challenges of this nature.

Issues of equity must be addressed. Programmes need to build in fee-relief provisions so that children who come from financially or geographically disadvantaged backgrounds can participate. No gifted children should be refused access to an appropriate programme because their parents are unable to pay for the services provided. We have a responsibility to find ways in which we can reach gifted children from low socio-economic areas, who are experiencing a double disadvantage.

In conclusion, the Australian Primary Talent Search has been embraced enthusiastically by those working in the field of gifted education in Australia, as an integral element in the process of identifying the needs of gifted students. It has been endorsed by the state government of Victoria and included in its 'Bright Futures' policy document (Australian Department of Education, 1999). Not only has it assisted parents and schools in meeting the educational needs of gifted students, it has also yielded a wealth of information and informative data, and raised many issues for further investigation of the needs of gifted students, which GERRIC hopes will guide the educators of tomorrow in assisting high ability students.

Appendix 1: Education in the UK

- **Organisation:** There were 10.1 million pupils in 34.6 thousand schools in the UK in 1999/2000. The types of schools included nursery, primary, secondary, non-maintained mainstream, special maintained, and pupil referral units. Total educational expenditure in the UK is estimated to be £38.4 billion. The Department for Education and Skills (DfES) has overall responsibility for managing the UK education system.
- **Age range for compulsory schooling:** five to 16 years.
- **Key elements of the curriculum:** The school curriculum is based on the national curriculum (www.nc.uk.net/home.html), which aims to establish standards and entitlement to learning for all pupils, and to promote continuity, coherence and public understanding. The national curriculum in England is different from the national curricula in Scotland, Wales and Northern Ireland. The *core curriculum subjects* in primary schools are English, mathematics and science. The other, *non core foundation subjects* are science, design and technology, information and communications technology, history, geography, art and design, music and physical education.
- **Assessment stages:** The national curriculum is organised on the basis of four key stages:

	KEY STAGE 1	KEY STAGE 2	KEY STAGE 3	KEY STAGE 4
Age	5–7 years	7–11 years	11–14 years	14–16 years
Year groups	Years 1–2	Years 3–6	Years 7–9	Years 10–11

At the end of each key stage pupils are assessed by statutory tests. Other, non-statutory, examinations are as follows:

- The General Certificate of Secondary Education (GCSE) is the principal means of assessing pupil attainment at the end of compulsory secondary education. It is offered by independent 'awarding bodies' according to nationally agreed criteria.
- GCE A levels are two-year study courses normally taken by students after they have completed their GCSE examinations. They are normally taken at the age of 18 and demand more individual, in-depth study than GCSEs.
- Advanced Supplementary (AS) qualifications are taken in conjunction with GCE A levels, as a means of broadening the curriculum beyond the confines of a three-subject course.
- General National Vocational Qualifications (GNVQs) are designed to develop skills needed for work in a broad occupational area. They exist at three levels: Foundation, Intermediate and Vocational. In order to complete GNVQ units, students have to undertake projects and thereby build a portfolio of 'evidence'.

- **Gifted students:** In March 1999 the UK government published a policy statement, *Excellence in Cities* (www.standards.dfes.gov.uk/excellence) (see Chapter 8). In September 1999 the gifted and talented strand of *Excellence in Cities* was introduced into some schools, and this provision will be extended to others. Among many initiatives designed to improve inner city schools and the performance of their pupils, new 'World Class' tests in mathematics and problem solving were proposed.

Excellence in Cities has also initiated project 'Xcalibre' (www.xcalibre.ac.uk), which will offer challenging opportunities to gifted students through its website. Furthermore, a grant has also been provided for the development of a network of Advanced Maths Centres (www.npt.org.uk), initially in *Excellence in Cities* areas, to enable gifted mathematicians in Year 6 to take GCSE mathematics before entering secondary school.

- **Other initiatives:** Education Action Zones (see Chapter 8) are set up in response to applications from groups of around 15 to 25 schools and their partners. Applicants describe how they plan to raise standards, and set themselves demanding targets for improvement by means of new activities. Each Zone receives a grant from the DfES as a baseline and a further sum in return for funds raised from private partners. Each zone is run by an Action Forum, and managed by a project director.

Appendix 2: Education in the USA

- **Organisation:** There are private and public schools in the United States, each governed independently by a local board of education. The public school system comprises approximately 15,000 school districts. The federal government does not play a major role in education governance, nor in funding for schools. The responsibility for education is delegated to the states and local school boards. For that reason, there is significant diversity regarding how US schools operate and what materials they use. Schools are organised in a variety of grade configurations. The most common are as follows:
  – Kingergarten to Grade 2 (K–2), Grades 3 to 5, Grades 6 to 8, Grades 9 to12;
  – Kindergarten to Grade 5 (K–5), Grades 6 to 8, Grades 9 to 12;
  – Kindergarten to Grade 8 (K–8), Grades 9 to12.
- **Age range for compulsory schooling:** In general, most states require students to attend school from age six to 16 years. However, the requirement varies from state to state with some states requiring children who are five years old to attend kindergarten.
- **The school curriculum:** Key subjects are as follows: language arts (reading, writing, spelling), mathematics, science, social studies.
  Other curriculum areas include the arts (music, art, drama), physical education and health, special education (programmes for students identified with disabilities), gifted education and, in high school, vocational education.
- **Assessment stages:** There is no national assessment plan. Student assessment varies in the 50 states. In general, students are assessed at ages eight, 10, 13 and 15 (Grades 3, 5, 8, and 10), but this varies by state and school district. The most commonly-used assessments are prepared by each state and their use is required in each school district. Nationally-normed, commercially-prepared tests are also used by local school districts.
- **Gifted students:** There is no national policy regarding gifted students in the US. Programmes vary from state to state and school district to school district. In general, gifted programmes in elementary schools are pull-out classes taught by a resource teacher with a special interest, or certification, in gifted education. In middle schools and high schools the courses are specialised for advanced students. Some examples would be algebra and geometry courses in the middle school and Advanced Placement courses in high school that enable the students to earn college credit.

Appendix 3: Education in Australia

- **Organisation:** There are 10,000 schools in Australia. The school year runs with the calendar year. In most states there are four terms, each lasting about 12 weeks.
- **Age range for compulsory schooling:** six to 15 years.
- **The school curriculum:** aims to help students fulfil their intellectual, social, artistic and career potential. Community involvement is encouraged, and the goal of education is seen as the provision of a skilled and flexible workforce. The scope and sequence of the curriculum is usually divided into stages or levels, each equating to two years of schooling.
  - Core curriculum subjects in primary schools are English, mathematics, social studies, science and technology, visual and performing arts (music, art, craft and drama), LOTE (languages other than English) and health (physical education and personal development).
  - Core curriculum subjects in junior secondary schools are English, mathematics, science, history, geography, computer studies, commerce, design and technology, foreign languages, visual and performing arts, physical education, personal development and health, with a choice of subjects being offered in the later years.
- **Assessment stages:** All states and territories have some form of assessment in the final year of schooling, the results of which are used as benchmarks for tertiary education. These differ widely, the only common examination being the International Baccalaureate – available in a small number of state and some private schools.
- **Gifted students:** Australia has no national policy on the education of gifted and talented children: provision varies. Most states and territories cater for gifted students within mixed-ability classes. Accelerated progression for gifted students is offered most consistently in New South Wales and Victoria. Attitudes towards identification procedures vary. Some states encourage standardised ability testing as well as subjective assessment; others do not.
  - New South Wales has established Opportunity C (OC) classes in primary schools and Selective High Schools to cater for gifted students. Testing for places is optional and occurs in Year 4 for the OC classes, and Year 6 and Year 10 for the Selective High Schools.
  - The New South Wales Board of Studies offers university-level Distinction Courses for secondary school students who have completed at least one subject early for Higher School Certificate (the end of Year 12 examination).
  - In South Australia, there are three special interest high schools for Students of High Intellectual Potential (SHIP). Six primary schools have ability-grouped programmes for academically gifted students. A pilot project giving gifted secondary school students access to courses at Flinders University has been initiated.
  - In Victoria there are 17 secondary schools offering an accredited Select Entry Accelerated Learning Program, which allows students to complete their six years of secondary schooling in five. The schools vary in the number of subjects in which they offer accelerated progress. Students in the senior years of schooling can be given access to an approved course at tertiary level, undertaken concurrently with their school studies.
  - In Western Australia, the Primary Extension and Challenge Program (PEAC) caters for students from Years 5 to 7 who achieve exceptional results in achievement tests. The secondary programme comprises the Academic Extension Program and the Arts Talent Program.
  - The Australian Primary Talent Search (APTS) is a national testing program for gifted primary school students, initiated by the Gifted Education Research, Resource and Information Centre (GERRIC) at the University of New South Wales (see Chapter 9).

Appendix 4: Equivalent year groups and grades in the UK, USA and Australia

STUDENTS' AGE (YEARS)	YEAR GROUP (ENGLAND AND WALES)	GRADE (USA)	YEAR/GRADE (AUSTRALIA)
5-6	Year 1	Kindergarten	Kindergarten
6-7	Year 2	Grade 1	Grade 1
7-8	Year 3	Grade 2	Grade 2
8-9	Year 4	Grade 3	Grade 3
9-10	Year 5	Grade 4	Grade 4
10-11	Year 6	Grade 5	Grade 5
11-12	Year 7	Grade 6	Grade 6
12-13	Year 8	Grade 7	Grade 7
13-14	Year 9	Grade 8	Grade 8
14-15	Year 10	Grade 9	Grade 9
15-16	Year 11	Grade 10	Grade 10
16-17	Year 12	Grade 11	Grade 11
15-16	Year 13	Grade 12	Grade 12

Note: the shaded areas indicate non-compulsory provision.

References

AEU (1999). Assessing higher levels of attainment in mathematics at key stage 2. University of Leeds Assessment and Evaluation Unit, unpublished report for QCA.

AGHION, P. and HOWITT, P. (1998). *Endogenous Growth Theory.* Cambridge, MA: MIT Press.

AMERICAN COLLEGE TESTING (1995). *EXPLORE.* Iowa: ACT.

AMERICAN COLLEGE TESTING (1997). *The Standards for Transition.* Iowa: ACT.

ARCHAMBAULT, F. X., JR.,WESTBERG, K. L., BROWN, S. W., HALLMARK, B. W., EMMONS, C. L., and ZHANG, W. (1993). *Regular classroom practices with gifted students: Results of a national survey of classroom teachers (RM 93102).* Storrs, CT: The National Research Center on the Gifted and Talented, University of Connecticut.

AUSTRALIAN COUNCIL FOR EDUCATIONAL RESEARCH (ACER) (1985). *Progressive Achievement Tests.* Victoria: ACER.

AUSTRALIAN COUNCIL FOR EDUCATIONAL RESEARCH (ACER) (1987). *Tests of Reading Comprehension.* Victoria: ACER.

AUSTRALIAN DEPARTMENT OF EDUCATION (1999). *Bright Futures: A Guide for Strategic Action to Support Gifted Students 2000–2005.* Victoria: Community Information Service for the Gifted Education Section, Department of Education.

BAKER, E. L., and O'NEIL, H. F. (In press). 'Technological fluency: Needed skills for the future'. In: O'NEIL, H. F. and PEREZ, R. (Eds.), *Technology applications in education: A learning view.* Mahwah, NJ: Erlbaum.

BALANCED ASSESSMENT (1998). *Balanced Assessment Packages.* Parsippany, NJ: Pearson Learning, Dale Seymour Publications.

BELL, A. and BURKHARDT, H. (1997). *Mathematics Tasks and Balanced Assessment: A Framework.* Nottingham: Shell Centre for Mathematical Education.

BLAKEMORE, S. J. and FRITH, U. (2001). The implications of recent development in neuroscience for research on teaching and learning, ESRC, Teaching and Learning Research Programme, p. 59.

BROWN, A. and DOWLING, P (1999). *Doing Research, Reading Research.* London: Falmer Press.

BURTON, L. (1986). *Thinking Things Through – problem solving in mathematics.* Oxford: Blackwell.

BUSINESS PLANNING AND RESEARCH INTERNATIONAL (2000). World Class Tests in mathematics and problem solving for 9 and 13 year olds. Unpublished research report prepared for the DfEE and QCA.

CAZDEN, C., COPE, B., FAIRCLOUGH, N., GEE, J. P., KALANTZIS, M., KRESS, G., LUKE, A., LUKE, C., MICHAELS, S., and NAKATA, M. (THE NEW LONDON GROUP). (1996). 'A Pedagogy of Multiliteracies: Designing social futures'. *Harvard Educational Review,* 66(1), 60–92.

COOPER, B. and DUNNE, M. (2000). *Assessing children's mathematical knowledge: social class, sex and problem-solving.* Buckingham: Open University Press.

DEARING, R. (1994). *The National Curriculum and its Assessment: Final Report.* London: School Curriculum and Assessment Authority.

DEPARTMENT FOR EDUCATION AND SKILLS (2000), *The Standards Site: gender and achievement* (http://www.standards.dfee.gov.uk).

DETR (1998). *Index of Local Deprivation, A Summary of Results*. London: Department of Environment, Transport and Regions.

DfEE (1999). *Excellence in Cities*. London: DfEE (now DfES) publications.

EDUCATION QUEENSLAND (2000a). *New Basics Project Technical Paper*. Brisbane: Education Queensland.

EDUCATION QUEENSLAND (2000b). *Queensland State Education 2010*. Brisbane: Education Queensland.

ELWOOD, J. (2000). 'Examination techniques: issues of validity and effects on pupils' performance'. In: SCOTT, D. (2000). *Assessment and Curriculum*. London: JAI Press.

ELWOOD, J. and MURPHY, P. (2000). Gender and performance at 14: tests, tiers and achievement. Unpublished paper, presented at the International Association for Educational Assessment, Israel.

FRAENKEL, T. (2000). Gender differences in the attractiveness of the distractor 'none of the above'. Unpublished paper, presented at the International Association for Educational Assessment, Israel.

FRASIER, M. M., MARTIN, D., GARCIA, J., FINLEY, V. S., FRANK, E., KRISEL, S., and KING, L. L. (1995). *A New Window for looking at Gifted Children* (RM 95222). Storrs, CT: The National Research Center on the Gifted and Talented, University of Connecticut.

FULLAN, M. (1993). *Change Forces: Probing the Depths of Educational Reform*. New York: Falmer Press.

GALL, D., BORG, B. and GALL, J. (1996). *Educational Research – an Introduction*. New York: Longman.

GALTON, F. (1869). *Hereditary Genius*. London: Macmillan.

GARDNER, H. (1983). *Frames of Mind: The Theory of Multiple Intelligences*. New York: Basic Books.

GERRIC (2000). *APTS Interpretation Guide*. UNSW, Sydney: GERRIC.

GOOD, C. D., JOHNSRUDE, I., ASHBURNER, J., HENSON, R. N. A., FRISTON, K. and FRACKOWIAK, R. S. J. (2000). 'Voxel-based morphometry analysis of 465 normal adult human brains.' *Neuroimage*, 11 (5), S607.

GRAY, K. R. (2000). Metaconstruct of the Rich Tasks. Unpublished manuscript, New Basics Branch, Education Queensland, Brisbane.

GROSS, M.U.M. (1999). 'Small poppies: highly gifted children in the early years.' *Roeper Review*, 21(3), 207–14.

HALL, E.G. (1983). 'Recognizing gifted underachievers.' *Roeper Review*, 5(4), 23–25.

HANSEN, J.B. (1992). 'Discovering highly gifted students.' *Understanding Our Gifted* 4(4), 11–13.

HARRIS, S., KEYS, W. and FERNANDES, C. (1996). *Third International Mathematics and Science Study: First National Report, Part 1*. Slough: NFER.

HARRIS, S., KEYS, W. and FERNANDES, C. (1997). *Third International Mathematics and Science Study: Second National Report, Part 1*. Slough: NFER.

HMI (1992). *The education of very able children in maintained schools: a review by HMI*. London: HMSO (now TSO).

INTERNATIONAL SOCIETY FOR TECHNOLOGY IN EDUCATION (ISTE) (1998). *National Educational Technology Standards for Students*. Eugene, OR: ISTE.

JACKSON, N. E., and ROLLER, C. M. (1993). *Reading with young children* (RBDM 9302). Storrs, CT: The National Research Center on the Gifted and Talented, University of Connecticut.

JACOBS, J. C. (1971). 'Effectiveness of Teacher and Parent Identification of Gifted Children as a Function of School Level.' *Psychology in the Schools* 8(2), 140–142.

JOHNSON, P. and REED, H. (1996). *Two Nations? The Inheritance of Poverty and Affluence*. London: The Institute of Fiscal Studies.

KENNARD, R. (1996). *Teaching Mathematically Able Children*. Oxford: National Association for Able Children in Education (NACE).

KENTUCKY DEPARTMENT OF EDUCATION (2001). *Draft Descriptors of the Grade 5 Mathematics*. Frankfort, KY: Kentucky Department of Education.

McGAW, B. (1996). *Their Future: Options for reform of the Higher School Certificate*. Sydney: Department of Training and Education Coordination.

MACKIE, L. (2001). 'APTS: What's the point?' *GERRIC News – Summer 2001*.

MARKET DATA RETRIEVAL (MDR) (2000). Nation's k-12 schools make major gains in technology (press release). Available: http://www.schooldata.com/pr22.html.

MARLAND, S. P. (1972). *Education of the gifted and talented: Report to the Congress of the United States by the US Commissioner of Education*. Washington, DC: US Government Printing Office.

MARS (2000). *Balanced Assessment in Mathematics: An Annual Set of Performance Assessments for US Grades 3 to 10*. Monterey, CA: CTB McGraw Hill.

MISLEVY, R. J., ALMOND, R. G., YAN, D. and STEINBERG, L. S. (1999). 'Bayes' nets in educational assessment: Where do the numbers come from?' In: LASKEY, K. B. and PRADE, H. (Eds.) (1999). *Proceedings of the fifteenth conference on uncertainty in artificial intelligence* (437–46). San Francisco: Morgan Kaufmann Publishers, Inc.

MISLEVY, R. J., STEINBERG, L. S., BREYER, F. J., ALMOND, R. G. and JOHNSON, L. (1999a). 'A cognitive task analysis, with implications for designing a simulation-based assessment system.' *Computers and Human Behavior*, 15, 335–74.

MISLEVY, R. J., STEINBERG, L. S., BREYER, F. J., ALMOND, R. G., and JOHNSON, L. (1999b). Making sense of data from complex assessments. Unpublished paper presented at the 1999 CRESST Conference, Los Angeles, CA.

MULLIS, I.V.S., MARTIN, M.O., GONZALEZ, E.J., GREGORY, K. D., GARDEN, R.A., O'CONNOR, K. M., CHROSTOWSKI, S. J. and SMITH, T.A. (2000). *TIMSS 1999: International Mathematics Report*, International Association for the Evaluation of Educational Achievement (IEA). Boston, USA: Boston College.

MURPHY, P. (1995). 'Sources of inequality: understanding students' responses to assessment.' *Assessment in Education*, 2 (3), 249–70.

MURPHY, R. (1982). Sex differences in objective test performances, *British Journal of Educational Psychology*, 52, 213–219.

MURPHY, R. (1988). *Social closure. The Theory of Monopolisation and Exclusion*. Oxford: Clarendon Press.

MYFORD, C. M. (1999). Assessment for accountability vs. assessment to improve teaching and learning: are they two different animals? Unpublished paper presented at the conference of the Australian Curriculum, Assessment and Certification Authorities, Perth.

NATIONAL COMMITTEE ON SCIENCE EDUCATION STANDARDS and ASSESSMENT (1995). *National Science Education Standards.* Washington, DC: National Academy Press.

NATIONAL COUNCIL OF TEACHERS OF MATHEMATICS (NCTM) (1980). *An Agenda for Action: Recommendations for School Mathematics of the 1980s* (p.18). Reston, VA: NCTM.

NATIONAL COUNCIL OF TEACHERS OF MATHEMATICS (NCTM) (1989). *Curriculum and Evaluation Standards for School Mathematics.* Reston, VA: NCTM.

NATIONAL COUNCIL OF TEACHERS OF MATHEMATICS (NCTM) (2000). *Principles and Standards for School Mathematics.* Reston, VA: NCTM.

NEALE, M. (1999). *Neale Analysis of Reading Ability (3rd Edn).* Victoria: ACER Press.

NEWBOULD, C. A. and SCANLON, L. A. J. (1981). *An analysis of interaction between sex of candidate and other factors.* Cambridge: Teacher Recruitment and Development Unit (TRDU).

OLSON, L. (Ed.) (2001a) 'Executive summary: Seeking stability for standards-based education.' In: 'Quality counts 2001: a better balance: standards, tests, and the tools to succeed.' *Education Week*, 20 (17), 11 January, 8–9.

OLSON, L., (2001b) 'Overboard on Testing?' In: 'Quality counts 2001: a better balance: standards, tests, and the tools to succeed.' *Education Week*, 20 (17), 11 January, 23–30.

OLSON, A. and LOUCKS-HORSLEY, S. (Eds.) (2000). *Inquiry and the National Science Education Standards: A guide for teaching and learning.* Washington, D.C.: National Academy Press.

OLSZEWSKI-KUBILIUS, P. (1994). 'Talent search: a driving force in gifted education.' *Understanding Our Gifted*, 6 (4), 1, 8–13.

ORLOFSKY, G. F. and OLSON, L. (2001). 'The state of the States.' In: 'Quality counts 2001: a better balance: standards, tests, and the tools to succeed.' *Education Week*, 20 (17), 11 January, 86–8.

PEGNATO, C.W. and BIRCH, J.W. (1957). 'Locating gifted children in junior high schools: a comparison of methods.' *Exceptional Children*, 23, 300–4.

PELLEGRINO, J. W., JONES, L. R. and MITCHELL, K. J. (1999). *Grading the Nation's Report Card.* Washington, DC: National Academy Press.

PITMAN, J. A. (2000). Senior certification: a new deal. Unpublished paper presented at the twenty-seventh annual conference of the International Association for Educational Assessment, Rio de Janeiro.

PITMAN, J. A., MATTERS, G. N., and O'BRIEN, J. E. (1995). An exploration of validity and reliability that tolerates distinct privileges: standardisation and contextualised judgments. Unpublished paper presented at the twenty-first annual conference of the International Association for Educational Assessment, Montreal.

PITMAN, J. A., O'BRIEN, J. E., and McCOLLOW, J. E. (1999). High-quality assessment: we are what we believe and do. Unpublished paper presented at the twenty-fifth annual conference of the International Association for Educational Assessment, Bled, Slovenia.

QUEENSLAND BOARD OF SENIOR SECONDARY SCHOOL STUDIES (1996). *The Road to Certification: The Queensland System.* Brisbane: Queensland Board of Senior Secondary School Studies.

RAGHAVAN, K., SARTORIS, M. L. and GLASER, R. (1998). 'Why does it go up? The impact of the MARS curriculum as revealed through changes in student explanations of a helium balloon.' *Journal of Research in Science Teaching*, 35, 547–67.

RENZULLI, J. S. (1971). 'The identification and development of talent potential among the disadvantaged.' *Contemporary Education*, 46(3), 122–25.

RENZULLI, J. S. (1973). 'Talent potential in minority group students.' *Exceptional Children*, 437–44.

RENZULLI, J. S. (1978). 'What makes giftedness? Reexamining a Definition.' *Phi Delta Kappan*, 60(3), 180–84, 261.

RENZULLI, J. S. (1988). 'A decade of dialogue on the three-ring conception of giftedness.' *Roeper Review*, 11(1), 18–25.

RUDDOCK, G. (2000). *Third International Mathematics and Science Study Repeat (TIMSS-R): First National Report. (DfEE Research Report 234.)* London: DfEE.

SCHAUBLE, L., GLASER, R., RAGHAVAN, K., and REINER, M. (1991). 'Causal models and experimentation strategies in scientific reasoning.' *Journal of the Learning Sciences*, 1, 201–38.

SCHMIDT, W. H., McKNIGHT, C. C. and RAIZEN, A. (1996). *Splintered Vision: An Investigation of US Mathematics and Science Education.* Washington, DC: US National Research Center.

SCHOOL REFORM LONGITUDINAL STUDY (SRLS) (1999a). *The Classroom Observation Scoring Manual.* St Lucia: The University of Queensland.

SCHOOL REFORM LONGITUDINAL STUDY (SRLS) (1999b). *Theoretical Rationale for the Development of Productive Pedagogies.* St Lucia: The University of Queensland.

SCHUMPETER, J. (1969). *The Theory of Economic Development.* Oxford: Oxford University Press.

SHEFFIELD, L. J., (Ed.) (1999). *Developing Mathematically Promising Students.* Reston, VA: National Council of Teachers of Mathematics.

SHEFFIELD, L., BENNETT, J., BERRIOZÁBAL, M., DEARMOND, M., and WERTHEIMER, R. (1995). 'Report of the Task Force on the Mathematically Promising.' *News Bulletin*, 32, December. Reston, VA: NCTM.

SHUTE, V. and GLASER, R. (1990). 'A large-scale evaluation of an intelligent discovery world: Smithtown.' *Interactive Learning Environments*, 1, 55–77.

SHUTE, V. and GLASER, R. (1991). 'An intelligent tutoring system for exploring principles of economics (333–66)'. In: SNOW, R. E. and WILEY, D. E. (Eds.). *Improving inquiry in social science.* Hillsdale, NJ: Erlbaum.

SIZER, T. (1992). *Horace's School: Redesigning the American High School.* Boston: Houghton Mifflin.

SMITH, R. A., MATTERS, G. N., COSIER, I. L., and WATSON, D. L. (1999). *Reinventing Years 10–12 in State Schools: A model of multiple learning pathways for new times.* Report to the Strategic Policy Branch, Education Queensland.

STERNBERG, R. J. (1985). *Beyond IQ: A triarchic theory of human intelligence.* New York: Cambridge University Press.

STERNBERG, R. J. (Ed.). (1994). *Encyclopedia of intelligence* (Volume II). New York: Macmillan Publishing.

STERNBERG, R. J. (2000). 'Successful intelligence: a unified view of giftedness'. In: VAN LIESHOUT, C. F. M. and HEYMANS, P. G. (Eds.). *Developing Talent Across the Life Span* (43–65). Hove, UK: Psychology Press.

STIGLER, J.W. and HIEBERT, J. (1999). *The Teaching Gap: Best Ideas from the World's Teachers for Improving Education in the Classroom.* New York: Free Press.

STOBART, G., ELWOOD, J. and QUINLAN, M. (1992). 'Gender bias in examinations: how equal are the opportunities?' *British Educational Research Journal*, 18, 261–76.

SWAN, M. and SHELL CENTRE TEAM (1984). 'Problems with Patterns and Numbers' and 'The Language of Functions and Graphs'. *Examination Modules for Secondary Schools*. Manchester: Joint Matriculation Board and Shell Centre for Mathematical Education. (Revised, Nottingham: Shell Centre Publications, 2000).

TERMAN, L. M. (1916). *The Measurement of Intelligence*. Boston: Houghton Mifflin.

TERMAN, L. M. (1925). *Genetic Studies of Genius: Mental and Physical Traits of a Thousand Gifted Children*. Stanford, CA: Stanford University Press.

TIMSS (1997). *Many Visions, Many Aims* (Volume 1). Dordrecht, The Netherlands: Kluwer Academic Publishers.

TROTTER, R. J. (1986). 'Three heads are better than one.' *Psychology Today*, 20, 56–62.

TUCKER, M. (2000). Personal communication.

UNICEF (2001). *The State of the World's Children*. New York: UNICEF.

UNITED STATES DEPARTMENT OF EDUCATION (1993). *National Excellence: A Case for Developing America's Talent*. Washington, DC: United States Department of Education, Office of Educational Research and Improvement.

UNITED STATES DEPARTMENT OF EDUCATION (1997). *Introduction to TIMSS: The Third International Mathematics and Science Study*. Washington, DC: US Department of Education Office of Educational Research and Improvement.

WAXMAN, B., ROBINSON, N. M., and MUKHOPADHYAY, S. (1996). *Parents Nurturing Math-talented Young Children* (RM 96230). Storrs, CT: The National Research Center on the Gifted and Talented, University of Connecticut.

WESTON, S. (2000a). *1999 Kentucky Elementary School Performance and Poverty*. Frankfort, KY: Kentucky Association of School Councils, July.

WESTON, S. (2000b). *1999 Kentucky Middle School Performance and Poverty*. Frankfort, KY: Kentucky Association of School Councils, July.

WESTON, S. (2000c). *1999 Kentucky High School Performance and Poverty*. Frankfort, KY: Kentucky Association of School Councils, July.

WHITE, B. Y. and FREDERIKSEN, J. R. (1998). 'Inquiry, modeling, and metacognition: Making science accessible to all students.' *Cognition and Instruction*, 16, 3–118.

WIGGINS, G. (1991). 'Standards, not standardisation: evoking quality student work.' *Educational Leadership*, 48(5), 18–25.

Index